More advance p

THIS WAY UP

"*This Way Up* is a treasure and a map, both at once. Cathrin Bradbury takes the reader on a trip to 'three-quarter life,' where love, art, and family become more meaningful than ever. A hilarious and unputdownable story of creativity, romance, and never-ending possibility."

—Elizabeth Renzetti, bestselling author of *What She Said*

"Bradbury details in graceful prose the uncanniness of considering one's life in retrospect, capturing the wisdom and surprise of a liminal state where "past and present" are more like neighbors than distant relatives. Sensitive and self-aware, this is a captivating meditation on what makes a life."

—*Publishers Weekly*

"Equal parts sharp-eyed and tender-hearted, Cathrin Bradbury has written a sly meditation on the wild ride of aging. *This Way Up* is both memoir and map—a navigation tool through the sticky stuff of life: friends, family, loss and love."

—Katrina Onstad, award-winning author
of *Stay Where I Can See You*

"Bradbury offers a deeply felt and insightful map that takes us through love, loss, family, sickness, heartache, joy and e-bikes as we enter our third act."

—Don Gillmor, award-winning author
of *Breaking and Entering*

"The triumph of this book is that it articulates and celebrates the everydayness of life, what Bradbury herself describes as the "lifelong craving for dailiness." . . . Treat yourself to *This Way Up*. It is a touching, engaging—and *true*—story of a life worth living."

—Joseph Kertes, award-winning author of *Last Impressions*

"Cathrin Bradbury has pioneered a delicious new form of autobiography that somehow manages to be both hard-nosed journalism of the everyday and stream of consciousness tone poems to a life still unfolding. *This Way Up* hits a sweet spot on an unlikely new Venn diagram that includes Carl Jung, Elizabeth Strout, David Sedaris, Sheila Heiti, and Martin Amis. With a journalist's tenacity and a standup comic's sense of timing, Bradbury, in her wandering way, gets right down to the unruly heart of the matter"

—Jason S. Logan, author of *Make Ink:*
A Forager's Guide to Natural Inkmaking

"I loved this funny, wise and honest memoir! Cathrin Bradbury creates a deeply personal map of her life, cracking herself open in surprising ways—it made me rethink my own relationship to ageing."

—Morwyn Brebner, award-winning creator of *Rookie Blue* and *Saving Hope*

"*As we head into the last quarter with death creeping at every thought, where do you put the fear?* So ponders Cathrin Bradbury in her compelling new memoir THIS WAY UP. With razor sharp clarity, sober detachment, and self-deprecating humour, Bradbury takes us on her own journey of unmapping and reclamation. Beautifully written, intimate and wise, *This Way Up* is a literate and loving testament to being human."

—Rod Carley, award-winning author of *RUFF*

Select praise for
THE BRIGHT SIDE

"Anyone who has had their life completely gutted and rewired will adore this family story. Bradbury's dark humour and gloriously upbeat voice makes it the perfect antidote to a tough year. I loved it!"

—Plum Johnson, bestselling author of *They Left Us Everything*

"In a spirit reminiscent of the great Nora Ephron, Cathrin Bradbury finds the funny in her own failings and the humour in heartbreak with her razor-sharp prose. *The Bright Side* reminds us when things get messy and painful, laughter is as important as light."

—Jessica Allen, *The Social*

"It is rare for a memoir to be very funny and unwaveringly honest. But Cathrin Bradbury's *The Bright Side* is brilliantly both. You could (quite correctly) call *The Bright Side* charming—but only if you also point out that it is smart, beautifully written, and mercilessly clear-eyed on the subject of what time has in store for us all."

—David Macfarlane, author of *Likeness*

"This warm, chatty memoir . . . serves as both a meditation on family and friendship and a love letter to Toronto and its colourful media characters."

—*The Globe and Mail*

THIS WAY UP

ALSO BY CATHRIN BRADBURY

The Bright Side

THIS WAY UP

*old friends, new love, and
a map for the road ahead*

CATHRIN
BRADBURY

VIKING

VIKING

an imprint of Penguin Canada, a division of Penguin Random House Canada Limited

Canada • USA • UK • Ireland • Australia • New Zealand • India • South Africa • China

First published 2025

Viking, an imprint of Penguin Canada
A division of Penguin Random House Canada Limited
320 Front Street West, Suite 1400
Toronto Ontario, M5V 3B6, Canada
penguinrandomhouse.ca

The authorized representative in the EU for product safety and compliance is Penguin Random House Ireland, Morrison Chambers, 32 Nassau Street, Dublin D02 YH68, Ireland, https://eu-contact.penguin.ie

LIBRARY AND ARCHIVES CANADA CATALOGUING IN PUBLICATION

Title: This way up : old friends, new love, and a map for the road ahead / Cathrin Bradbury.
Names: Bradbury, Cathrin, author
Identifiers: Canadiana (print) 20240506944 | Canadiana (ebook) 20240506952 | ISBN 9780735248632 (softcover) | ISBN 9780735248649 (EPUB)
Subjects: LCSH: Bradbury, Cathrin. | LCSH: Older women—Biography. | LCSH: Older people—Biography. | LCSH: Aging—Popular works. | LCGFT: Autobiographies.
Classification: LCC HQ1063.7 .B73 2025 | DDC 305.26/2092—dc23

Cover, cover illustrations, and book design by Jennifer Griffiths
Typeset by Erin Cooper

Printed in the United States of America

1st Printing

Penguin
Random House
VIKING CANADA

To Kelly and Mary

Let's go out and fight the storm
—Margaret Atwood, "Blizzard"

Something tells me:
You will never do anything more vital,
more profound, more perfect or more
Necessary than what you are doing right now.
—Gwendolyn MacEwen,
"Sunlight at Sherbourne and Bloor"

CONTENTS

one

MY MAP

I WAS GOING TO NEED a map.

It was one of those 3 a.m. ideas, with the undistracted clarity only the smallest hours of the day can provide. I usually grabbed my phone from the bedside table to act on these thoughts instantly, often to my sorrow. My brain lagged trying to understand why the pour-over kettle I'd ordered arrived thumb-sized, until I read the fine print: *Perfect for your dollhouse.* My first and only foray into vibrators—recommended by *The New York Times*'s Wirecutter, so what could go wrong?—was the Magic Wand, a name that suggested wizardly sprightliness, not the police truncheon that showed up at my doorstep. (Fine print: *For women who like a lot of power.*)

"Measure once, measure twice, measure three times," said my brother Tim, a carpenter, after the fridge I'd ordered didn't fit in the allotted space. It was my first new appliance post-divorce. "Don't you know that's the cardinal rule before you buy anything?"

"No, Tim, I don't know that rule. Do you know the rule that you blow-dry your hair from back to front, with the brush held above your head?"

So I took care when I ordered my map. Obviously, I couldn't buy a map to where I was headed. Even my deliriously clear 3 a.m. brain understood that any journey into the land of old is uncharted territory. Although the signposts were everywhere.

The way I could open a bottle of cranberry juice one day and the next day I could not—a skill unlikely to return. Discovering on a hiking trip with friends that at least half of them had to pee more often than I did and being *triumphant*. I mean, it made the whole trip. Walking into a table or chair—furniture that had always been there; no one was moving it around in the night—and finding myself apologizing to a footstool. How my adult children had begun to speak to me in exclamation marks. *"Mom! Be careful!"* *"Mom! What are you doing!"* Being eulogized when you're sitting right there. *"Remember the time Cathrin . . ."* The transporting joy in the smallest moments: a twenty-year-old running, legs high, in the cold winter morning; a lone bird calling at night, too early for spring. The liberation from the tyranny of things that "matter." Not apathy, but that time's too short or moving too fast—the onrush of time that you don't have time for. Or perhaps that time, unexpectedly, has become too vast for petty things to get a handhold. I try to put myself in the way of time when it expands like that, when this newfound space of time makes it an ally instead of an enemy.

These changes are so gradual you almost miss them, until they become who you are now. A person with sudden ineptitudes, who triumphs in petty victories, worries much less than she used to, and is parented by her children. Yet she has found the supernatural ability, at last, to inhabit a moment—and bumps into furniture. The accumulation becomes the evidence that you're in new territory.

If I couldn't get a map to my future, I could at least find one that showed me where I'd come from. Lately, where I'm going and where I've been felt more and more like the same question. When you're a kid, time's so slow the recent past is ancient history—you can't wait to move beyond it, to be nine when you're seven. But at sixty-eight, my past and present had a newfound fluency. The older I got, the closer the places from my childhood became, until we walked around arm in arm like long-lost friends.

At 3:15 a.m., I paid Amazon $5.95 for a street map of the place where I was born and then lived for the first six years of my life. St. Catharines is a Southern Ontario city next door to Niagara Falls. When I was a child it was in its boom days, but now it was one of those slumped midsize cities with most of its industry long gone and much of its downtown boarded up. Writers often describe how the locations of their stories choose them, how the first thing they know about a book is where it will be set. For some reason, St. Catharines was choosing me. Other places have more resonance in my life: Grimsby, the town we moved to after St. Catharines and where I spent my formative years. Toronto, the city I'd made my home after university and had stayed ever since. The North, where I've traveled since I was a child and where my imagination lives. But it was the little thought of, barely remembered town I was born in nearly seven decades ago that had become a glint in my mind, demanding my attention.

The first problem with my new map when it arrived two days later was that the type was the size of salt. I needed a magnifying glass to see anything, and even then, it was impossible to read the street names. "Take a picture with your phone and expand it," said my friend Ellen from up the street who excelled at life hacks. But the second problem was that I didn't know what I was looking for because, as I said, I left St. Catharines very young. My mind held clues like runes: "Don't play in the gully"—what gully?—and the excited feeling of crossing a high bridge across a deep expanse I couldn't find on the map, and running running running with dozens of kids on the cul-de-sac where our post-wartime bungalow sat. Our street name, I hadn't forgotten, was Argyle Crescent. I liked the sound of living on a crescent, swinging my legs on the curve of the moon. But I had no idea where to find it on my map.

My older brother Tim and his wife, Nancy, both grew up on our street in St. Catharines—Tim really did marry the girl next door—so I invited them over to my house, ostensibly for their son's birthday celebration but really to look at my map. Before they arrived, I spread it over the table we'd soon be eating off. It took up the whole table.

"Come in, come in!" I said, swinging open the front door. "It's windy out, isn't it? Let me take your jackets. Watch the step." We hugged and kissed in the entryway, but all I could think about was my map, waiting to be introduced like an unexpected guest. "Right this way," I said, waving them into the dining room.

My map did not disappoint. It was the hit of the party. It took me places, too, the way only a map can.

two

WHERE ARE WE NOW?

IT WAS ON THE AFTERNOON the bike courier ran into me that I first began to think the questions I'd been trying to ask myself weren't about identity—who am I now?—but about location: Where am I now?

My biker was one of about a dozen couriers taking a break on the sidewalk, the shiny black coolers that delivered food from somewhere in the city to somewhere else resting briefly at their feet. There was plenty of room for me to get by as I walked toward them. And then—

"Ouch! What? Sorry!" I apologized when he stumbled into me. This man was maybe twenty-five. His job was to zigzag around cars, people, and other e-bikes at top speed, balletically in sync with the flow of city streets. He had the peripheral vision of a bald eagle, yet he'd failed to track my presence. It's not that I'd expected the couriers to notice me. I'd been invisible since I was fifty-three; that's an old story, and not this one. But the day the courier stumbled into me like I was a fire hydrant or a construction cone—an obstacle to be gotten around—was when I understood that I wasn't just invisible but had dropped out of the picture altogether.

I began to wonder if my own peripheral vision had become an inconstant companion—bumping into furniture—because I'd lost my coherence with the world. For most of life, everything around you joins together into a remarkably detailed story that you take in at a glance as you move through space. A story you're at the center of—the hero of, even. In my fantasy life, and my writing life too, the main settings are detailed and brightly colored. What was happening on the grassy patch just off the sidewalk where the courier had collided with me? I don't know. It didn't figure. I've never explored the borderlands of a scene. The edges fade to gray; they're not central to the story, peripheral.

Until the center shifted. Now there was this sly version of me that was in another story, as if the main story was going one place and I was skulking toward another. At sixty-eight, between the end of middle age and the beginning of old age, I started to wonder about what was going on over there, in the unformed gray areas. Instead of trying to get back into the main plot, my lifelong preoccupation, I began to ask: What's it like here, in the trickly borderlands?

Where am I now?

"I need a pen," said my brother Tim, pushing away my magnifying glass as he bent over my map on the dining room table. This was very Tim, this perfect vision at seventy-five. He gave the impression of supreme ease in the world, whether or not that was true (he'd say it wasn't). Also taking command of the map, like a surgeon about to operate, me the nurse with the scalpel.

I have four siblings, fifteen years from top to bottom—a full generational spread—and the flow of knowledge and experience moved from the eldest to the youngest and back up again. Laura is eight years older than me. I've always been able to see what was ahead because of Laura. At seventy-six, she has life changes coming, and how she behaves in the face of those will be my own steady guide. Tim comes after Laura, and next is David, the closest to me in age by two years, which gives us a bond neither of us needs to talk about. I'm fourth, a privileged position partly because of this backward-and-forward perspective, and partly because it's a less prominent place in a family of five, not a top-billing spot, which means more time to myself. Even in the fullest happy moments, surrounded by people like my siblings, who I love—or maybe especially in those moments—I'm checking the exits. Then comes Ann, seven years younger than me and fifteen years younger than Laura. Ann was in a big transition as she approached sixty, the same way I'd been at her age: kids launched, husband decamped, new man arrived (except I didn't have that last part). After our parents died, we siblings sat in the same room where Tim and I were now studying my map and agreed that even without Mom and Dad to bind us, we would remain close. It was a decision instead of a happenstance of history. But our history is something only we have. We are five. I am one of five. It's as much who I am as anything.

I put the pen in the hand Tim reached out behind him.

"Here's our street." He circled a speck on the map several times.

"His vision's incredible, isn't it?" said Nancy, who referred to Tim as "your brother" when he irked her. She soon found the park at the end of our street that used to be the gully, forbidden "because people lived in there." It was thought to be a dangerous place, she told me, but likely they were just men out of work.

"Right." Men sitting on the ground in a circle took shape in my mind. Remembering what happened was easier when you could see where it happened. "They burned campfires."

"I never noticed how hemmed in St. Catharines is." I stood back from my map to take in the big picture, and wondered if the city's geography gave it a locked-in energy, and that's why it had presented itself so powerfully to me at 3 a.m. The gray and mighty Lake Ontario bound the city to the north, the brow of the Niagara Escarpment to the south, Twelve Mile Creek west, and the Welland Canal east. The canal's twenty-seven miles of locks and water allowed ships to descend the three hundred feet between Lake Erie and Lake Ontario, from the second highest to the lowest of the five Great Lakes.

"What's all the excitement?" My son Kelly swooped his son over the map like a plane, to the baby's delight. "Your grandfather"—I was speaking now for the benefit of our grown-up kids, who'd joined us at the map—"and your *great* grandfather," I said to the baby, "would take us to watch the lakers and ocean liners pass through the canal." I tapped the map with my finger, wishing I had a pointer. It wasn't often that the thirty-year-olds gathered to hear what I had to say.

The workings of the huge locks that made the ships go up and down was something, but it wasn't only that. Sailors from everywhere in the world would stand on the ocean liners' decks as they passed through. They'd watch us wave and not wave back. That's when I got my first inkling that there was something bigger out there, the way those sailors looked at us without smiling, like they'd seen better.

"Look! We're on the map." Sam, Tim's middle son and a carpenter like his father, found the location of the new family compound on the southeast corner. Sam rented an apartment in my house and was turning a backyard shed into a hut for me to write in. He would soon leave to work with Tim and David to build what would become a multi-generational home in Fonthill, Ontario, very near to St. Catharines. I called it the Commune, and though it was still a work in progress, it already had a bigger sense of itself than this dot on the map showed.

It was time for dinner, so I folded up my map and we laid

out the food on the same table. "Happy Birthday to you," we sang in rousing harmony. The baby didn't have words yet, but his eyes blazed with the candles he helped blow out. We cut the cake, and Tim's youngest son, whose birthday we were celebrating (Tim has three boys, born within three years of each other more than thirty years ago; my own children, Kelly and Mary, were born a couple of years later), complained that his older brother didn't sing his name. "He sang, 'Happy birthday to—' and he wouldn't sing my name."

The genius of siblings to torment each other is usually invisible to everyone but them. I didn't speak to my brother David for two days over a disputed bag of potato chips; we were both in our sixties at the time. So when Tim's sons and my own began to horse around with a stuffed orange-and-black puffin that belonged to the baby, throwing it high in the air and then jumping up and chest-bumping to see who could catch it first, I was ready for this game to go wrong. The words I meant to come out of my mouth in my living room with the puffin flying to the ceiling and the young men reaching up and the late-day sun making their red hair glow like fire, everything lit, were "Look out. Be careful."

"You four are exactly the same as when you were tiny kids," I said instead, because the eight of them were there, the boys and the grown men. They all paused to grin at me.

"Of course we are," they said, and threw the puffin up again.

—

After everyone left, I put things back in order, slowly and thoughtfully. I was happy with the stir my map had caused. The excitement to see the borders of our hometown and how we'd lived within them convinced me I'd been right to buy this map. I'd gotten answers to my questions too: the name of the wide bridge, and where our street was. But I was pretty sure the map was telling me something else that I hadn't thought to ask.

I laid it out again, smoothing it like a tablecloth with wide sweeps of my hands from north to south and east to west. What I noticed this time was not just how hemmed in St. Catharines was but me too. I've carried the idea of my big life since I was seventeen, and I lived it, traveling all over, often on my own, unafraid of whatever came next. But the truth was there on the map: I'd moved two inches, to the other side of Lake Ontario. From St. Catharines, you can see Toronto on a clear day. It's that close.

"My puny life," I said to Ellen. It was the day after the party, and I was walking to the park with Ellen and her giant dog, Sally. "Right there on the map for all to see."

"There's nothing wrong with staying put," Ellen said, then grabbed me by the arm. "Run!" She pulled me into the revving traffic with only three seconds to go before the light turned red.

To cross the street with Ellen was to experience the unknowable. Sometimes there were fourteen seconds left and she'd insist we wait. One day she'd walk two blocks in broad daylight to cross at a stoplight to avoid jaywalking, and the next night, wearing a black coat with Sally the color of twilight beside her, she'd dart across the dark road when there was a stoplight only steps away. I knew Ellen better than anyone, and I never knew what she was going to do. Take a job or leave it, love a man or leave him, borrow my ice bucket for her party, *as we'd agreed she would,* or run out and buy a new one minutes before I dropped mine off.

"You're precipitous as hell," I said, yanking my arm out of her hand when we got to the other curb.

"I don't know why you'd see staying still as a passive choice. Cyclones and snow squalls can churn intensely in one place." Ellen was from Winnipeg, one of the coldest cities in the country, where reading the weather wrong could have life-or-death consequences. As it is with most Canadians, winter was her inner landscape as well as the outer. We're way up there on the globe; our country cracks into pieces the farther north it goes, like doomed ice floes headed off-map.

"Am I the squall in this story?"

"I'm saying a lot goes on, and a lot has gone on, in a life that looks circumscribed. Yours included."

When I got home from my walk with Ellen, I went back to my map, still open on the table. I wasn't ready to fold it up and put it away. I grabbed the pen and circled my place. *Here I am.*

My map did have some answers about where I was and where I'd been. Tim and Sam had even seen their future, what was next for them was there on the edge of the map. Maybe a map had ideas about where I was going too.

three

ON THE ROAD, PART 1:
BETWEEN HERE AND THERE

I GOT LOST ON MY way to meet the curator of McMaster University's map library. The irony of that escaped me for some time. It was a very minor adventure to travel on the GO commuter train from Toronto to the Hamilton campus, about an hour and a half with one transfer from train to bus. And yet.

"You didn't tap in," said the GO Train officer when I handed him my transit card. He squared his feet and crossed his arms like a stern letter *A* as he stood over me in my seat.

"I tapped something." I was as amiable as the August sky was blue, but I was filled with fear at my crime. "But sorry, I can tap again now."

"It's too late for that."

The officer became sad as he clicked open a pen and began to write what might have been *Les Misérables* for the time it took him to finish what I presumed was a ticket.

I decided to look calmly out the window as he did this, although I knew the fine for bilking the transit system could be four hundred dollars. More troubling, how was I going to bravely set out for whatever came next when I couldn't master the train to the next city over? The worry beads of travel—was I on the right train? would it stop at the right place? would I make my connection?—were already clicking over in my head, and now this.

He handed me a thirty-five-dollar fine: *Did commit the violation of failure to show a valid ticket when directed.* I briefly protested that the system was at fault, not me, before he moved down the car to the next passenger and I settled myself into my backward-facing window seat. When the train jolted, that bump of relief that said I was finally in motion, I texted my friend Gillian.

Are you here or there, I asked her, because I hoped to meet soon and I didn't know if she was in Ontario or Quebec, the two places where she spent most of her time. I didn't notice the connection between my question about my friend's whereabouts and my own circumstances, both immediate and philosophical. But coincidence is magnanimous. It doesn't care if I'm paying attention.

I woke up wondering am I here or there, Gillian texted back. She was a Buddhist scholar and thought about these things. *a good Buddhist is always "here" but I haven't got the hang of that—yet!*

I feel I'm ALWAYS somewhere between here and there.
I gave a furtive look at the GO officer's back. *I guess I have a ways to go.*

I also have a ways to go. but the Buddhists might say that the mindset behind "a ways to go" is part of the problem.

This text ended with a tiny emoji that I tried to expand because I wasn't sure if it was praying hands or someone meditating cross-legged, in the same way that a squirrel sitting in profile with his tail arced behind him can look like a rooster from a distance. That's a bit of a brain twister because you're not expecting to see a rooster on the sidewalk in the middle of the city, and then the mind adjusts for probability, but more slowly than it used to, giving you time to think about roosters and squirrels and the ways they are different.

What about "and miles to go before I sleep"? I wrote. My back was toward the engine, giving me the feeling of being pulled away against my will from where I had just been. I was going backward into the future, lulled by my streaming view of trees moving in the opposite direction, blurring until they were one continuous tree, light winking through. The Japanese word for it, *komorebi*, describes both a quality of light through trees and the feeling of an unrepeatable moment. And also to be in that moment.

It's a paradox. There's conventional reality and ultimate reality. In the former we're moving, in the other we're not. Moving and not moving at the same time felt like the direction I'd been headed for quite a while. Perhaps not the Buddhist way but a way.

On the McMaster campus an hour later, Google Maps showed me turn by turn how to get to the map library, where the voice said, as it does: "You have arrived at your destination." Which was an idle patch of grass. I walked in circles, looking at the dot on my phone, and then stood still.

"Excuse me," I said to a woman walking by. "Do you know where you are?" I reached out my phone to her. "I can't find where I'm going on the map."

She peered into my outstretched hand. "You're in the exact opposite corner of the campus from where you want to be."

I opened my arms to the verdant quad. "But Google Maps brought me here." Did my voice come out too high? When I lost where I was going, I could feel lost in all ways.

"Don't worry, it happens," she said kindly, and then she delivered me like a missing letter to the Mills Memorial Library, where Saman Goudarzi was waiting in a large low-slung room rimmed with every kind of globe. An all-blue sphere mapped the earth's water; groovy planets circled an orange George Jetson–style globe. There was a beach ball globe, as well as a celestial globe with a small earth encased in a Lucite graphic of the stars beyond. I was entering charted territory.

Saman leaned over the maps she'd laid out on the library's counter. She was taller than I expected, very tall, but otherwise just the way she'd looked in her picture, with brown eyes and brown hair parted down the middle and tied back. At thirty, she was the youngest map curator in Canada, and the first of three map people I would talk to. None of them seemed to mind that my interest in maps was more existential than geographical. Mappers are tremendous enthusiasts of the journey, whatever form it takes.

I'd chosen Saman as my first map expert to help me answer my first question—not where was I going but where had I come from. There was an almost forty-year gap in our ages, but her youth did not make the past uninteresting to her. She loved thinking and talking about the meaning of location, and often had visitors from the area who, like me, were curious about what maps could tell them about their analogue past, the snail trail of where they'd been. For my visit, Saman had chosen from the hundreds of thousands of maps in the library's collection to show me the story of where we lived, starting with the never-ending province of Ontario. Drive from east to west, and three days later you're still in Ontario. England could fit within its southern tip, where I'm from; France and Spain could tuck into the rest. Saman's historic maps showed the evolution of my old stomping grounds: there was the gradual creation of St. Catharines, on the underside of Lake Ontario, and Grimsby, twenty minutes to the west, where we moved when I was seven.

"My personal favorites are the fire-insurance maps,"

Saman said, "like this one of Hamilton." Where we were now, twenty minutes west of Grimsby, and where my father worked for the same company his whole life. Saman called the fire-insurance maps "place-based storytelling," and I could see why. The detail was incredibly granular, showing the direction of each street, the building material of the houses on it, and the location of every fire hydrant—all of which would affect your insurance rates.

"These fire maps are Google's precursors. Google has created a very usable product that has made most people's lives easier"—she smiled woefully at me for a moment; I'd told her about Google abandoning me on the way to her library—"but its goal is to create profit for its shareholders. What they want you to see becomes the only way you see space."

Saman flipped through a book of British maps of Ontario from the 1800s, with the rod-straight concession lines that still exist. If the history of maps is a story of power and exploitation as much as it is of wayfinding, then these maps were a precise example. "British citizens were given property within those concession lines in exchange for building roads and farming. But what they also did was render the Indigenous inhabitants between those lines invisible."

Today's maps are more democratic, or at least some of them. Data maps can be tools for resistance, another kind of power, mapping first-aid resources within a war zone or places of sexual harassment for women to avoid. The

Covid-19 pandemic was a boon to health maps. Saman told me that mapping in the future "will be more a tool to visualize information for any part of human life, and less a road map from here to there."

Here to there. That placeification of time again: there I was, past place, and here I am, present place. "I like being here or there, but not in between, where things tend to go wrong," I told Saman, still thrown by my failure to tap in.

When we finished our tour of the maps, Saman walked me to the bus, perhaps worried I'd lose my way. She was a loper, as tall people often are. I trotted beside her and asked her questions, partly to slow her down.

"Why maps?" I wanted to know.

"I was going to be a farmer but decided I wanted something that didn't require so much physical work." It was a professor who'd set her on a new course. He told her "place is just space with meaning." I'm accelerating her journey from farmer to mapper, but we agreed that sometimes a good line from a memorable teacher can turn you in a new direction.

Sandra Rechico's studio was easier to get to from my house, a pleasant walk south through Toronto just as the fall leaves began sprinting from the trees like a starter pistol had gone off. Sandra was an artist who'd spent much of her life drawing maps, and I'd told her on the phone how my paper map of St. Catharines had provided unexpected happiness.

"Unlike Google Maps, which makes us anxious," she said, "your map of St. Catharines gave you the big picture." Instead of this turn and the next turn that we spend so much of our lives following on GPS. "Maps ask us, 'What am I trying to locate? How did I get here?' They describe what is valuable to you and what is less valuable. It's super personal." I decided I had to meet her.

Her studio was a tiny cement rectangle in a building of similarly tiny artist studios, but it didn't feel like a box once you were inside, partly because of the light coming down from a long window in the corrugated tin roof. The skylight was covered by gauze, softening the gray cement walls to the color of winter clouds. Floor-to-ceiling metal shelves held neatly labeled artworks, and like Saman, Sandra had brought some of them out to help tell her own map story.

She'd been drawing maps to make sense of things since she was a little kid, she told me. Later, as an artist, she became fascinated by how she moved through space. For five years, from 2003 to 2008 (just around the time Google Maps was taking hold), she started to keep track of where she was in the city.

"For thirty-one days each May, I wrote down exactly how I moved around Toronto, then came home and used colored dots and black graphic tape to chart my routes on the wall." She showed me photographs. "You can see from the thickness of the tape on the wall the places I went to over and over, like the hardware store for art supplies." From those taped routes, she created black line drawings of the city that looked like asymmetrical spiderwebs. Some of them were framed and propped against one wall of her studio. It was like looking at the nervous system of where I lived.

For several years, Sandra was part of a public mapping project called Map It Out, which traveled from Berlin to Cardiff, Wales, to Providence, Rhode Island. The project asked participants a simple question: "How did you get here?" And then asked them to map their answers. One woman used a single swoop of her pencil, with a small x at each end, start to finish, here to there. Someone drew a bus. Another made a detailed drawing of a taxi navigating roads and traffic signs. One simply wrote a list of street names.

"Once, in Providence, when we asked, 'How did you get here?' a man drew a map of Syria." His home had been bombed, and he'd ended up in Providence because he had no choice but to leave his country and immigrate to the US. "I thought that was a very interesting response to the question."

I'd recently made my own map, I remembered as Sandra told me this story. It was part of a workshop called a blanket ceremony at CBC News, my final job in journalism. The session was designed to make participants not just think about but also locate within themselves the genocide of Indigenous Canadians as they were robbed of their land, forced onto reserves and into residential schools, and killed through disease (cholera-ridden blankets, for one) and murder. At the beginning of the workshop, the Indigenous facilitators asked each of us to make a quick map of seven places that were important to us, however we chose to draw it. As they had in Sandra's "How did you get here?" project, people made lists, drawings, or labeled squares. At random times as the class continued—it lasted several hours—we were asked to tear those places out, starting with the one that mattered most.

None of us looked at each other as we ripped our papers because it felt shameful to have everything you loved and understood taken from you: your town, your neighborhood, maybe where you worked. That exercise stayed with me—the loss of place, and the theft of place. Our legacy as Canadians.

"My map centered around my house," I told Sandra, and one by one, I lost the rooms where my family and I had lived. "It was almost physically painful to tear out those pieces from my map."

"Yes," she said. "Maps show you what matters. That's the personal part."

Sandra eventually began to map her experience of various cities around the world, charting her movement through them with that black graphic tape on the walls of local galleries, as she'd done each May in Toronto. She liked putting maps on walls because you saw the faults, the bumps and cracks. "Maps have errors inherently, so an uneven wall is a very concrete expression of that." When the exhibit was over, she would ask someone at the gallery, often the curator, to dismantle the tape and send it to her. How that person did that, and what they sent, she left entirely to them. Sandra placed the tiny pieces of art one by one in my hands. Each seemed to contain its essential city. *Two Weeks in Paris* was a palm-sized ball of glinting silver and black tape loosely bound and almost weightless. It felt like I had the City of Light in my hand. Another power of the map, not of exploitation but of energy.

As I prepared to leave, Sandra paused at the door and looked at me. "We've met before, years ago," she told me. "I was dating someone you worked with." I looked at her too, and suddenly saw her from back then, tall and blonde and curious at a crowded party. People I'm meeting for the first time I've often met before, sometimes only for a moment, and then they come back as in a spiral, the past and the present together again. It happens more often than you'd think.

We reminisced a little about that party and the man she used to date, and before I set out for home, I asked Sandra my last question: What could a map tell us about the future?

"Now that's the thing I'm not so sure about," she said. "Maps show potential, but they don't answer what's coming next."

I took a break from my map quest for a manicure at a midtown salon. Except even there maps came up, the way experience starts to mimic what you're writing.

"What do you call an intersection like this that's not symmetrical?" I asked the manicurist as she held my hand in her own. "The way it jogs on the east–west axis?" I'd just navigated the jog, stopping and starting as I dodged bikes and scooters and mopeds and cars to get to my appointment.

"I think you call it a jogged intersection. I've seen two terrible accidents here," said the manicurist as we looked out the salon's floor-to-ceiling windows. "Blood everywhere," and I silently thrilled because I'd been right about the risky intersection. The conversation moved to how dangerous the world had become in general, when the woman beside me, waiting for her own manicure, said she thought the world was less dangerous, not more. Then she told a story about travel irons.

"I'd carry my travel iron in my hand as I walked around Paris in 1972 and threaten to hit the men harassing me." She brandished an invisible travel iron, which I could see perfectly because I'd traveled with one too. In fact, I'd taken one to Paris in the exact same year. (Maybe this woman and I had had another of these path-crossings back then, and here we were sitting next to each other forty years later at the nail salon.) I'd never used my iron as a weapon against the grown men who followed seventeen-year-old me for blocks, whispering obscenities. It was never much use at all, really. But the possibility, at least, of ironing seemed essential in 1972.

"Travel iron?" the manicurist asked with mild interest. She wore her hair in a high ponytail, and it bobbed as she looked from one of us to the other. The woman and I went off about traveler's checks, airmail paper—and especially, once the excitement over the travel irons had settled down, the never-ending folding and unfolding of maps. I told her I was writing about maps and the age we were now.

"Maybe this conversation will be in your book," she said.

"Travel irons," I said. "How could it not?" (She later tracked me down, Karen was her name, to tell me that she had recently traveled back to Paris and, "at sixty-five found I no longer required a travel iron.")

On that trip to Paris, with my travel iron and my paper map of Europe, which I marked with my own colored dots showing where I'd been, I also carried the *Lord of the Rings* trilogy in my backpack. I found it a terrific travel guide of the spirit. (I still do, to the collective agony of almost everyone I know. We all have our private pleasures: true crime, historical romance, CNN, NFL. Go ahead and cast the first stone.) Each of Tolkien's books began with a map, launching eighty years of world-building maps in fantasy books: *The Lion, the Witch, and the Wardrobe*, *The Golden Compass*. Even those dark rabbits in *Watership Down* had a map. Throughout the entire eight-season, seventy-three-episode run of *Game of Thrones*, my daughter, Mary, watched the two-minute opening sequence, which panned across

three-dimensional maps of the fictional world, never jumping ahead. "I like to start by seeing where we are," she said,
her eyes on the screen.

"Forests are named, cities plotted, seas charted. It's as if
fantasy maps set out to deny the unreality of the worlds they
depict." The final stop on my highly selective tour of
Canadian map-thinkers was Robert Rouse, a professor in the
English department at the University of British Columbia.
His specialty was medieval geographical imagination, and
his path to maps also started young. "Most of my family
lived in England, but I was raised in New Zealand. Which is
a place in the middle of nowhere." As a kid, he saw the world
through maps, wondering where he was and where his family
was, and how you got from one to the other.

"In *The Hobbit*, when Bilbo Baggins leaves Bag End"—
leaves his easeful home against his better judgment for an
unknowable adventure, a worry I'm more sympathetic to
at sixty-eight than I was at seventeen—"his road may go
'ever on and on,' except we know exactly where, because
Tolkien gives us the map." Almost all these fantasy maps
are "sneaky replicas of the dominance of Europe, with the
east and the west full of threatening strangers," Robert told
me on the phone. "Racial and geographical ideologies
underpin the fantasy genre."

I asked Robert my question about whether maps could
tell me where I was going, and he described how he began

one of his courses at UBC. The Hereford Mappa Mundi is the largest extant medieval map, at about four feet by five feet. It was designed not to find a direction but to give spiritual and human perspective. East, not north, is at the apex, where the Garden of Eden sits on the edge of the world. Drawn on calf skin, it includes about five hundred cities, towns, people, animals, and biblical and mythological scenes with fantastical creatures. There's a lot going on in this map, so it's not surprising that Robert's students missed what he thought was one of the most important things about it: the letters on the north, east, south, and west otherwise empty borders outside of the busy map were M-O-R-T.

"Death is where maps are headed. That's the place we're all traveling to."

A map to my cemetery plot. My least favorite destination. Not to age, but to the end of age. The end of my age. And here so soon, before I've barely set out for the craggy peak of seventy? Let's give death a moment, then grab a shovel and bury it deep.

Philip Larkin wrote his death poem, "Aubade," when he was fifty-five; he died eight years later, at sixty-three. In my experience, it's somewhere in those years that your mortality asserts itself. *Most things may never happen: this one will.* There are more beautiful lines in Larkin's poem, but the unadorned truth of that one made it inescapable. We're

all going to die, and sooner than we'd like. Sooner than
I'd like. Death creeps into every thought like a spider I'd
like to kill.

"You have high mortality salience," said Tim the Jungian
(not Tim my brother, although they were sometimes inter-
changeable in my dreams), whom I saw most Tuesday eve-
nings, as the light slowly left his office and dusk came in. My
mortality and my mother were steady topics (what else?),
especially since my mom had died. On that day, I ran and ran
to get to her while she was still alive—the nurse had said,
"Come now"—but I was four minutes late. Entering her
room was like standing in the eye of a hurricane, which I had
done many years before on a family holiday to the Caribbean.
The storm was raging like an angry husband, hurtling
branches, sand, and water at 150 miles an hour against our
duct-taped sliding glass doors, and then it stopped. We left
our semi-submerged room on the beach and stepped outside
into a colossus of absence. I reached out my arms to touch
the hushed stillness at the center of the storm, the same way
I wanted to reach out to my mother. Not to her body, which
she had unmistakably vacated, but to the silent void I felt all
around me as I stood next to her bed. It wasn't dying he
wanted to get out of, Larkin said. It was being dead. And
then life rushed in, the storm on the other side of the hurricane's eye raged back. But I'd visited the empty place, and
that certain sense of nothingness stayed with me like a thin,

echoey tap on a bongo drum by a droopy-eyed beatnik. What waits *tap tap* off map *tap tap* is annihilation *tap tap*.

"Doesn't everyone fear death?" I knew Tim's answer. He'd told me many times. I just didn't believe him.

"No," he said. "Some people don't."

"Do you fear death?"

"I do not." By now, it was dark enough for him to reach back and turn on the light behind him. "Life and death are two parts of the same whole. One contains the other. We're all dying all the time."

"Sure, sure." I squinted. "I'd just rather not do it." I didn't like the light in my eyes. Two living people ebbing away in front of each other while death lounged at the door was enough illumination for one night.

I kept my final piece of torn paper from that Indigenous blanket exercise, the last place remaining on my own map. It was a drawing of the newly laid stone path from my house to the writing hut that my nephew Sam was building. "Path," said the word beside the rough circles I'd drawn in pencil. The path that leads from my home of twenty-five years, with all the history inside it, to my new hut, with no history but perhaps a future I barely understood. I suppose at the time that "path" was the thing that mattered least to me, but now I'm not so sure it wasn't what mattered most.

four

I HAVE A HUT IN TORONTO, AT THE FOOT OF THE GARDEN PATH

I had a farm in Africa, at the foot of the Ngong Hills.

KAREN BLIXEN, *Out of Africa*

———

I HAVE A HUT IN Toronto, at the foot of the garden path
doesn't soar as a sentence. Changing an unused corner of
my backyard into a hut doesn't quite hold up to changing
an African river into a lake either, as Blixen did when she
first arrived in Mombasa, bending "her" land to her will.

But putting scale aside: like Blixen (nom de plume Isak
Dinesen), I imposed my ego on the landscape for all to see.
Because a ten-by-ten hut of one's own in a cheek-by-jowl
urban backyard was hard to miss. In fact, a ten-by-ten hut
in your backyard looks less like a private retreat than it
does a bold monument to ego. And that's before what happened when I started to use the hut.

—

The year of the hut was also the year I retired from four and a half decades of work as a journalist. My original idea for my retirement send-off, which I'd spent the summer planning, was that I'd set out for my own adventure as soon as the party was over. I'd disappear like Bilbo Baggins in "The Long-Expected Party," the first chapter in the *Lord of the Rings* trilogy, those books I'd carried when I left home for the first time. And maybe would again, for what might be the last. That Baggins and Blixen were my companions as I got ready for my trip was unexpected, but whoever wanted to come along, that was fine. My dad would join us too. "I wish I'd gone farther" he'd said before he died at ninety-four, drifting in time to his modest travels after his own retirement. "India! China—imagine that!" I did imagine it. I'd scoured the world for what freedom could look like after my life of toil: Crete for the winter, near a white-sand beach with blue blue water all around, or maybe a cottage with a view in Wicklow, Ireland, where I had distant cousins.

I planned these trips into the wide waiting world while at the same time Sam built a small garden hut, where I also intended to stay put and write. My work as an editor at newspapers and magazines had been in service to other people's writing, and I loved that, not least because it allowed me to stay behind the scenes. I'd hoped to be a writer when I began my undergraduate degree in English in 1974 (no one originally plans to be an editor). But big debt and slender opportunity—the hundreds of post-graduate creative writing programs designed to launch writers did not exist in the 1970s—helped me put aside that idea of myself. That and the very mundane sense that for most middle- and working-class people, especially if you didn't live in a big city, and prior to the leveling influence of the internet, to say out loud that you wanted to be a writer would be ridiculous. I did try to get hired by top magazines and newspapers when I graduated, with dashed hopes: men I knew got jobs as writers right out of school, women as secretaries and assistants to the male writers and editors. My own first post-university job was as an editorial assistant on a magazine called *Gifts and Tablewares*. It was not my dream job. The concept of gifts and tablewares eluded me, for one thing. Then there was the nature of the work: writing press releases about Lucite napkin rings was some distance from the multigenerational novel I was creating in my head. I wondered what was more humiliating: to have taken that job, giving up on my best hopes for who I might become, or to have been fired from that job a year later.

But if I was preemptively cautious at twenty-five, writing became a new and unignorable urgency when I turned sixty. Time moved much faster than I had understood. I feared I had wasted it. The path not taken in my twenties opened again in my sixties, like a shadow career waiting for its moment to come out. By the time I retired, I'd been writing for a few years, plonking down wherever to work in the vibrant quiet of the early mornings: the kitchen table, a corner of the living room. Unritualized, catch-as-catch-can. The hut was not just me taking myself seriously; it was me letting everyone else know I was doing that.

I look back in wonder at the cognitive dissonance that allowed me to pursue two motivating desires that were in direct opposition with each other. I was like Colm Tóibín's two-timing Jim in *Long Island*, who simultaneously planned his wedding to Nancy in Ireland and his life with Eilis in New York. *Jim, oh Jim. What are you doing, Jim?* But this is where life is lived, on the parallel track. My tracks shared momentum, at least. One outward, the other inward; one unbounded (because retirement is a huge life change that needs space to be experienced), the other hemmed in (because retirement is a huge life change that needs hunkering down to be understood). The two ideas for my future couldn't coexist for long. The mind bender was that I needed the hut, and the room it provided for contemplation, to make the decision about whether my future was on the road or in the hut.

The idea of the hut began when Gillian took a gardening course and was tasked to reimagine an urban landscape. "I'd love to use your backyard as my subject," she said. Since my divorce, I could find room in my head for the inside of the house or the outside of the house, but not both. The outside had been let go. On a bravely blooming March afternoon, with the white snowdrops and purple crocuses pushing through the frigid earth that smelled of cold, Gillian looked out at my mostly lawned backyard, which in Toronto without pesticides meant mostly dandelions, and said, "Let's dream."

"A pool here," I paced it out. I'd already bought and sold a secondhand hot tub because it was too much work and smelled of chlorine. But I was chasing an idea of serenity and ease as I prepared to retire from the grind of work. Pools and hot tubs seemed to suggest both.

"What about that shed." Gillian pointed to a small structure at the end of the lawn that my daughter, Mary, had made cheerful by painting all over with giant pink birds. Between the birds and the tall asters and black-eyed Susans my son, Kelly, had planted from seed as a teenager—my backyard was a modestly pleasing place to spend an hour or two.

"Maybe the shed could be something more?" said Gillian.

We let go of the unwise and unaffordable pool, but when Gillian showed me her completed drawing a few weeks later, with a lovely latticed structure in place of the shed, it occupied my mind for a long time before it occupied the yard.

"What are these?" I pointed to a row of trees drawn next to the little hut.

"Hornbeams," Gillian said. "Protecting you and blocking out the messy view of the hydro wires."

I might not have gone ahead if I hadn't found out that I was going to be a grandmother. "I have a surprise, mom," said Kelly when he FaceTimed me from Guatemala. I cried so hard I surprised both of us. Kelly couldn't stop laughing and I took a screenshot of our faces contorted in big emotion. On an earlier call, my son had said he'd like me to ease up on my baby agenda. "I do not have a *baby agenda*." "*Mom!* It's all you talk about. The truth is, we're not sure if we want kids." So this news was an unhoped for joy. "And you know what? When we move in with you"—we were all going to live together while he and his partner, Ivonne, found their feet in Toronto—"we figure you'll know all about raising kids." I dried my eyes. I'd longed for the arrival of a grandchild—Kelly was right about my baby agenda. But the baby's new life and my own new life, post-retirement, were coinciding in a timeline that was unexpected. I saw Crete wisping away like a handful of sand on the ocean wind. And not just Crete but my other post-retirement dream, to finally give birth to myself as a writer. I didn't yet feel the tug between being with the baby and being on my own, or know that my grandchild would outshine any desire to live my live more freely. That would come later. All I knew was that with a full house, I'd be working where I slept.

My nephew Sam had just returned from a trip out west, to bring his cousin home for urgent cancer care, and he had a lot of post-road energy as we stood in my yard considering the potential of the hut. He told me about a wolf in the road on the long drive home. It was a story of hope I wouldn't forget (eventually I asked to hear it again; I'll be sharing it later), and it made me feel optimistic about my new hut.

"What do you think, Sam?" I said as we surveyed the contents of the shed—one hand lawnmower, two rakes, four plastic plant pots, three old paint cans, and two bikes.

"A lot of real estate for a couple of rakes," said Sam.

"I'm thinking French doors here." I moved my arm in a sweeping gesture. "And can we take the point off the roof?"

Sam managed my expectations. One door might work, maybe a window on the side. No to the flat roof. "I'm just worried that no matter what we do, Aunt Cathrin, it's always going to be a tool shed."

The electrician arrived. "Everybody is doing these huts all of a sudden," he said. "I've wired three in the past month." Not everyone used them for late-life vocations. Some were guest huts or play huts for kids. My neighbor to the south was building a meditation hut; our huts would abut.

The electrician showed me a picture on his phone of the most recent hut he'd wired, a two-story prefab with a three-month waiting list. It was pretty.

"My tool shed will be just like that once it's fixed up," I said.

The electrician gave my sad-sack shed the up-and-down. "Nothing like," he said.

Karen Blixen was beset by questions as she trooped through her vast coffee plantation, bossing the twelve hundred workers she employed. Ditto me and my ten-by-ten hut. Existing shed or new prefab? (The latter, in the end.) Facing garden or house? (Garden.) Roof angle? (Sloping down to the north.) Paint color? (Dark gray outside, whitewashed inside.) Heating? (All the men I knew wanted wood stoves in their own imaginary huts. I did not.)

A hut needed a cement slab, which involved soil disposal bins, a mixing truck, and a four-person work crew. "Doing a lot of these huts, I hear," I said to the cement boss.

"These what?"

"Huts. You know. What we're building."

"I wouldn't know anything about that," he said, smoothing the fresh cement in broad, rhythmic sweeps with his pallet *swoosh swoosh swoosh.* "We call these shed slabs."

Sam worked long hours to build the hut. Kelly often held a flashlight for his cousin to see by after the sun went down. And then, just in time for my retirement party, it was finished.

I stood on my back stoop and looked out at the people I'd invited to celebrate my life of work. There were colleagues from the fashion magazine where I got my start in the cocaine-stoked, can't-spend-enough 1980s. And from my half a dozen other media employers as well—I had moved around a lot, not always by choice in the rough and diminishing world of journalism—all the way to the people from my final job at CBC News. We were together for what a French colleague called the "corridor *du panique*" of the Covid shutdown, the storming of the Capitol in Washington, the invasion of Ukraine, nuclear threats from Russia, and blazing forests and atmospheric rivers at home. Those years were the most punishing news cycle of my career. I wasn't sad to be leaving the job behind, even as I said goodbye to people I cherished and admired.

To mark the occasion, I'd bought a new blouse, silver-white satin and flowy like a cloud. Like my new weightless life. Laura, who'd paid for an oyster bar, and Ann, who'd flown in from Vancouver, made sure everyone had a drink before I made my toast to myself. Kelly, glowing like a sunset in a burnt orange sweater and rust tweed jacket, and Ivonne, in a glamorous black dress and pearl choker, held the baby between them. He was all in white and shining in the twilight.

At the back of the yard, behind my family and guests, was the freshly painted hut, and alongside it the four new hornbeam trees, where I'd strung fairy lights for the party. As I began to make my speech on my back stoop, close friends stood very near, looking up into my face, giving me courage and comfort. I'd spent hours preparing. I'd rented a microphone and speaker, to be sure I was heard. My brothers once told me, as I made a Mother's Day toast to ours, who'd died the year before, that it was "Too long. Sit down and be quiet."

"People pay money to hear me talk, you know," I lied to them then, but I'd since honed my style. Bilbo Baggins's audience had also hoped for something "short and obvious" when the loquacious hobbit made his own farewell speech, standing on a chair under an illuminated tree (because height and light are both important in speechmaking). I managed to say what I wanted to say. "Thank you, thank you everyone," I finished. I didn't have a magic disappearing ring that would let me vanish in a puff of smoke before my guests' eyes. My plan was to vamoose in the next couple of weeks. But even as my mind set out, my body had known better all along that my grand adventure would be the thirty-three steps along the stone path from the house to the hut.

A hut is not a house. This was the first thing I learned in the very short journey to the end of my backyard, which I've taken most days since my retirement, wrapped in a blanket— it's often chilly in the mornings—and holding a mug of coffee and the silver key to the hut door that was mine alone.

There were the sounds. From the house, the noises were of cars and ambulances and footsteps of laughing passersby. From the hut, it was rain, sleet, and wind, except it was as if the weather were happening inside the thin walls of the hut, not outside. It could be worrying, but it kept me alert. The birdsong was nice, the manic squirrels trying to dig through the roof less so. At the fronts of houses, people greeted each other loudly as doors swung open. In the back, the people sounds were solitary and slightly ominous: chopping, sawing, drilling, creaking, or sometimes, the alarmed voice of a child calling from his own backyard, "*Dad! Dad!*"

A house has momentum. So does an apartment, or anywhere people live. It's the go-go life. Guests arrive and leave, things are dropped off at the door, mail is delivered, garbage is taken away. In the hut, the only movement was of my own thoughts, as mysterious as the backyard sounds, but a mystery I needed to solve. That the word "hut" was taken over by marketing to mean something welcoming and fun—Pizza Hut, Sunglass Hut—was a misdirection. "Hut" comes from the old English *hydan*, to hide, cover, or conceal. It has a lot in common with the word "retire," which is from the French *retirer*, meaning to retreat or withdraw into seclusion. My discovery was that a hut was less a place to hide out than a place to find out what was hidden to you.

Deborah Levy found something similar in her London garden-cum-freezer shed, where she wrote her wildly wise three-volume *Living Autobiography*. Her books were among the few things I kept in my hut. It shunned decor. There was a small cot for napping, a white desk, and silver chair. On one of the whitewashed walls hung Jessie Oonark's *Power of Thought,* a drawing of a woman's face with a bright geometric halo radiating out from it. On another wall, a blue ink letterpress view of Grimsby from the escarpment. I did get my French doors, which looked north onto the row of hornbeam trees. A small window faced west to the house. From my desk in the tiny room, I could turn my head to look at either view.

"The squirrels"—Levy had her own squirrel action in her writing hut—"would suddenly turn their gaze towards me, as I sat alone in the shed. Although they appeared to be startled, I knew they knew I was there *before* they turned to look." She went on: "The things we don't want to know are the things that are known to us anyway, but we do not wish to look at them too closely."

When I retired, I believed that I was headed out there, wherever the map would take me. But the whole time I was thinking about moving outward I was building an inward future in my own backyard. I went somewhere I'd thought I never wanted to be again: to a small and enclosed space, a lot like the offices where I'd spent so much of my working life. A place, it would turn out, that was so private and contracted, it offered depths I had not plumbed or even discerned.

A hut is not a house, that was true. But it took building something of my own, across the smallest possible divide from a place I could and wanted to return to—my house, where my four-month-old grandson was thriving—to bring this home to me. Everything I needed was closer than I expected it to be.

I fantasized about my grandson being old enough to run to the end of the path and knock on the hut door. Yes, he knocks; he is a polite child. I thought about whether I could protect him from the world I was not yet ready to venture out into all over again at sixty-eight. I considered my own late birth as a writer, how to hold that next to the birth of another human being, and whether now was really the time to find myself in a hut in the backyard. And I felt the risk of new love.

I often forgot to turn the hut lights on in the dimming afternoon. As the day ebbed and the kitchen at the back of the house got brighter, I could see Kelly in my pink Marimekko apron, chopping vegetables for dinner. I locked the door of the hut with the silver key that was mine alone and headed home for dinner, my blanket over my shoulders. This hut was going to be too cold for the baby in the winter. I'd better get more blankets.

five

LISTLESS

THAT FIRST WINTER OF MY retirement, I tackled a bedroom closet stuffed with paper, the messy remains of a lifetime of work. I am a determined culler except when it comes to paper. It accumulates. Notes and clippings—clippings! as quaint a concept as a travel iron—business cards, letters, files marked "Ideas," that torn piece of paper with "path" written on it, paper clips, newspapers, and two stacks of Day-Timers, listing my daily tasks, going back twenty years.

On a cold and cloudless December afternoon, the sun so low in the sky it blinded me at eye-level, I spread the Day-Timers over my bed, and felt locked in, not only by the weather but by the relentless need to keep track. My lifelong craving for dailiness. It was then that an idea began to take shape—a revolutionary one, even, for me:

Maybe it was time to let go of the list. To pay attention not to what needs doing, but what is doing. To let the day have its own say about where it wants to go. Not to forge the path, but to follow it.

—

During my working life, I'd go to bed most nights thinking about the list I'd write in the morning, ticking off what I'd done the day before, writing down what I'd do next: my daily path in blue ink on lined paper. I made the day what it would be. I created it on the page. My work Day-Timers were ten by twelve, black and hard-covered. They meant business—I could see that right away as I flipped through them. They looked like I was planning the invasion of Normandy every single day. I followed a geographical battle plan: above the lines for personal reminders, numbered middle for tasks, with daily carryovers. Each entry was as comprehensible as division by zero, code-like clues whose meanings fade shortly after they're written.

My notebooks, post-work, are orange with a spiral spine, soft-covered, and smaller, at six by eight inches. The urgency of the list has lapsed in the orange book, although the entries, when I remember to make them, are equally gnomic.

1. *Cilantro.* That was easy enough. I likely needed some.

2. *Bag.* What bag? Whose bag? Where bag? Pick up my bag at the shoe repair, it came back like a pop of color on a dark suit. ("A bit sudden," as Kingsley Amis once described a man's sartorial daring.)

3. *When I go to the drugstore* is like the middle line of a haiku. I don't know where that task came from or where it's going.

4. Go through old Day-Timers.

Sometimes there'd be a scrawled thought at the bottom of the page in the orange book, to add to a story later, before I forgot. A year ago, a word or idea would return on command. Now just a faintness came back, like a damp sidewalk where yesterday's snow had been. I'd neglect to add context or attribution, so this part of the page was by an unreliable narrator. *Unadorned time. Ungainsayable. The way a man looks back at his locked car before he walks away. Tea towels too terrible to describe.* (That's American author Todd McEwen.) *I could have fixed the leak.*

I'd get lost in one of these notes for some time as my day expanded and contracted like a concertina. A list of five things took nine times as long to write because there were sixteen steps between moving from item one to item two. *I don't know what I do all day, but it takes me all day to do it—* someone said that. Where distraction used to be something to snap out of to get back to work, the wandering focus of my day was now where the action was.

As I lay on my bed—I love to be horizontal, especially to read and think—my old Day-Timers surrounding me like black cars in a funeral procession, I saw I'd written *Umberto*

Eco! on the "To Do" part of a page. Eco was the first famous writer I tried to conduct an interview with, in my first consequential job, when I was in my mid-thirties. The office where I worked faced busy railway tracks and trains headed for Union Station. My boss took me to the window one day and said, "If you don't get Eco, I'm going to tie you to those tracks." I believed her, so I called and wrote and begged him in every format possible. He eventually declined, in a telegram in the form of a poem, so I wrote a short story about that instead. (This was before the internet, and I've lost both the story and the telegram.)

My Eco episode came back to me right away, but there was another memory just beneath it that I couldn't quite recall. I lay on my bed and let the minutes wander by until the memory wandered in. It was like watching the sunrise; it took forever to surface, the hopeful rays brighter brighter brighter, and then pop, there it was, just above the horizon: Eco had a thing for lists!

"How, as a human being, does one face infinity? How does one attempt to grasp the incomprehensible? Through lists." This was Eco to the German magazine *Der Spiegel* in 2009, before literary essays on the beauty of the list bloomed like poppies in Provence. Eco had just published *The Infinity of Lists*, and he had curated a Louvre exhibition on the essential nature of lists in painting and literature. "Your eyes are so beautiful, and so is your mouth, and your collarbone ... One could go into great detail," Eco said about lists and love in that inter-view. And on death: "We have a limit, a very discouraging, humiliating limit: death." Lists have no limits, Eco said, "and, therefore, no end ... We like lists because we don't want to die." My black books did let me escape thoughts of death, and I thank them for it. I don't judge their shortsightedness. It's not nothing to accomplish so many things in a day. But lists are heuristic, shortcuts for thinking rather than actual thinking. They give the illusion of meaning because they matter a lot in the moment, and then they don't matter at all. Today will be pretty much the same as the day before and the day after. That's what an old list tells you. If I could do it over again, I'd find a way to do less. To think about what matters in the day I'm living, rather than writing a list of how to manage it. If that would have been possible. Likely not.

Thirty years later, stumbling around in the foothills of old, the list feels too flimsy to stand up to my quickly encroach-ing mortality. And yet, I can't quite let go of the impulse to account for myself. To compare and contrast where I've been and where I'm headed. Not a reckoning—I'm not interested in judgment. More like a tally. A tally roots inward; it looks beyond the moment. A tally says today will be a lot like yesterday. Only better.

six

A TALLY, PART 1: HAVE AND HAVE NOT

WHAT I HAVE:

1. I'm alive. So far. Samuel Beckett strode with an old friend through the gloriously sunny streets of London, New York, or Paris—the setting varies depending on who's telling the story—and exuded a feeling of joy, rare for the famously pessimistic Irishman. The old friend said it was the kind of day that made one glad to be alive. Beckett responded, "I wouldn't go that far."

2. Two grown children: Kelly and Mary. I count my blessings every day at my astounding good fortune to have these people in my life. Who could have dreamed it at seventeen?

3. One grandson.

4. One grandson's mother. No, I don't think of her that way! Or not only that way. Ivonne is a woman who is many things,

49

and many things to me, besides the mother of my grandson. But they are usurpers, these babies. "The baby's mother was here," said Gillian, and then we both heard it. The baby's mother, in that case, was Gillian's daughter. Not *my daughter was here*, but the *baby's mother was here*. One grandmother wrote that on a visit to her sick son and grandson, she gushed "My poor darling," as she ran past her feverish son to pick up the baby, only clocking her son's downcast face after it was too late. But this is how we loved you and love you still, our children.

5. One house. Now that my children have left, the house is my constant companion. But no matter how much you love a house—and I do, and often thank it for the steady way it keeps the rain and snow out and the warmth in—a house is still a construct, something built in space and also in your mind. Your love for a child is not a construct. It's a big realization when your children are infants, this fact that your love for them is not a story you're telling yourself, or writing about, or building. Love is real. Sometimes.

6. Four siblings. Laura, Tim, David, Ann. Try to remember those names—they'll be coming back. There are just four of them, it's not a Russian novel. Already, the brothers are arguing with me: Why are siblings number six on this list? Behind the house?

7. One honorary sibling. Nancy is the only in-law left since the rest of us divorced or separated, and she has many talents: school principal, athlete, empathic listener. She also created the Nancy Keenan Dinner, to be enjoyed alone, after the most stressful day: one bag of potato chips (not the small size) and one Manhattan. I recommend it.

8. Three nieces and four nephews. Adults now, and cousin-friends.

9. Two friendships for life. Although you don't know they are for life until you've lived for some time. "Friendship is promiscuous," said Hisham Matar, in an interview about his unforgettable novel *My Friends*. You can have many friends at once, he said, cheating on them, and they might last months, and they might last a lifetime. "Friendships are collaborative. They are works in progress." I've known Ellen since our thirties, and Meryl since we were six. Ellen and I walk and talk on parallel tracks, and occasionally our conversations intersect and we talk back and forth for a while. We're Grand Central Station, the way our talking tracks merge and separate. "We basically have the same conversation over and over," Ellen says every time. When her niece asked, "How long have you two been best friends?" we were both astonished. Our relationship is intellectualized; we don't go in for emotional ideas like best friends. Plus, we're two cold fish; our hands

are icy to touch. Meryl lives in a different city and has a different life from mine. Our friendship exists outside of time and place. We talk less often—sometimes not for months, and once not for twenty years. But when we do talk, we pick up where we left off. We're on the phone for hours, talking about books, as we have our whole lives (when we read Elena Ferrante's Neapolitan novels, we both felt Ferrante had written them precisely about us, and for us to read together), and grandchildren, a new topic, and most things in between. "We have survived," said Meryl. "You are my old friend. Like the song says, bookends." We're all heart—that's thanks to Meryl. We don't finish our sentences; our emotional fluency requires fewer words.

10. Many other dear friends and meaningful acquaintances. The meaningful acquaintances are sometimes easier to navigate because the history is lighter. The arena of the meaningful acquaintance is a very slender aspect of the past. With other dear friends, when you're sixty-eight, it's more profound and also more complicated. Take any pair of women with a fifty-year friendship under their belts, and there's been love and bloodshed, daily phone calls, and ten-year rifts. Book club. Say no more.

11. My bikes. I've ridden bikes since I was five and understood at once the freedom they brought, waving as I glided

past my parents. My first purchase with the earnings from my first job at thirteen was a twelve-speed blue Gitane; Meryl bought a red one and Arlene, our other best friend at the time, a white one. Our plan was to ride across Canada to write stories of the people we met, and we applied for a government grant to subsidize the trip. It was 1969, when they were giving away grants like flyers, so even though we were three fifteen-year-old girls looking for cash to run away from home, we were surprised when our application was turned down. My second bike, after the Gitane was stolen, was a silver Nishiki, which I've held on to since my early twenties, a miracle in the bike theft capital of Toronto. I remain a proudly self-propelled traveler. My bike keeps me on a continuum with that fifteen-year-old girl and the truths she held precious. (Although, as a woman of nearly seventy, what I mostly think about on my bike is staying alive.)

12. A new and unexpected vocation as a writer.

13. Some art I bought when I was finally divorced, at sixty, as a private and public expression of who I was. A lot of self-exploration is necessary when buying a piece of art. If you want to have a complete nervous breakdown when you're at the end of a marriage and trying to figure out who you are on your own, I suggest you buy a piece of art. Many of mine are portraits of women, like Oonark's *Power of*

Thought or Bradley Wood's *Lounging on Mies van der Rohe.* "Don't you think you have enough pictures of women looking out at you?" an art collector friend asked when I considered a third portrait. I didn't, though.

14. The essentials: computer; iPhone; my tunes, first on albums, then on cassettes, then on CDs, and now on my phone, mostly, and mostly on earbuds while walking.

15. One Jungian, who some weeks or months or years would be higher on this list and not after tunes. "Roshi cared deeply about me, or he deeply did not care about me. It was hard to know which," said Leonard Cohen about the monk he climbed to the top of the mountain for, and whose latrines he spent years cleaning. "The common element is something deep is going on in his relationship with Roshi," I said to Tim the Jungian as we talked about the connection between analysts and their clients. "Yes," he said. "You care deeply, and you also deeply don't care. But the deepness of not caring has its own substance."

16. One hut, a path to the hut, and a garden beside the path. Gardens used to make me anxious, with all that life teeming around. But then I met Elisabeth, an expert gardener whose idea it was to make the stone path and build a garden around it. I might have resisted further, until she said we would rim

the path with *gently nodding hellebores.* They have names like Ivory Prince (the palest white) and New York Nights (shades of black), and they do nod at me as I walk the path, and I nod back.

17. Optimism, an inherited condition my whole family suffers from. I long wished for an uncanny upbringing on a bleak moor. No such luck. We wake up happy. We're optimistic about getting old, too, which may help us age better. Positive views of aging result in improved performance on hearing tests and memory tasks, according to Yale psychologist Becca Levy. The author of *Breaking the Age Code*, Levy wrote about the need for an age liberation movement to acknowledge how we become more creative and productive later in life. "You can't create beliefs, but you can activate them by exposing people to words like 'full of life,' instead of 'grumpy or helpless' to describe older adults."

18. All the comes-with-age stuff. Experience. Elasticity of thought and feeling. I'm merging studies here, from Harvard to *The New England Journal of Medicine* to the University of Montreal and more, but they together report that this mental and emotional elasticity starts around sixty and continues until eighty. When we're younger, each hemisphere of the brain might be responsible for a particular type of information, and the two don't meet up. Old brains, on the other hand, recruit

right and left hemispheres at the same time, efficiently choosing the least energy-intensive path and cutting unnecessary information on the way. We get wise, is another way to put it. Better able to synthesize disparate views, less susceptible to absolute truths and black-and-white thinking. Both sides of the coin. At sixty-eight, I've attained the hard-earned and often best-kept-to-myself right to dispense advice.

19. Nosebleeds—*Mom! You're bleeding!*—and bruises. "Where'd you get that bruise?" someone asked their old mother. "The wind," she replied.

20. Pain. One morning you stand up and notice that something hurts. It's your feet. Rising from bed and standing on your own two feet sends knife twists of pain up your legs. It hurts your thumb to shake a hand. It hurts your shoulder to reach for a shirt hanging in your closet. Hips seize, knees buckle, jaws click. Your eyeballs are sore. Fingers gnarl like aboveground roots. Necks go out from looking left or right—from moving your eyes, not your head. The fascia, the protective film around muscles and joints and organs, like that thin white layer on a chicken breast, is wearing down; your insides are grinding against each other. "Everything hurts all the time," my mother said at ninety-one. After a while you don't talk about the pain, even to yourself.

21. Time. Ben, my financial adviser, puts my life expectancy at ninety-four. "Why, thank you," I said. "I do try to keep fit." But it's an actuarial calculation, not a compliment, arrived at through data on things like lifestyle, education, and location. Still: ninety-four. That's a quarter of my life coming up, and unlike the first quarter, which I mostly spent crashing around with an underdeveloped brain and overdeveloped personality, the final one will be—I hope—as a productive adult.

22. Legacy. Not of money or talent, but maybe, for my children and grandchildren, of a way to see the world. I'm still thinking about that.

What I don't have:

1. Old age. Not yet. Medicine defines young-old as 70 to 75; old 75 to 84; and old-old, 85 and over. It's wonderful how middle age keeps expanding, like a balloon that's going to burst. One magazine profile referred to comedian Larry David as middle-aged. He was 77 at the time of the article. The faster it approaches the further it recedes, the American Psychological Association reported. "At age 64, the average participant said old age started at 74.7. At age 74, they said old age started at 76.8." The study offered a bright side: the people who believed old age started later reported being less lonely, in better health, and feeling younger.

2. A job. After fifty-five years, since my first job picking cherries at thirteen to pay for that blue Gitane, I have retired from working under anyone else's bidding for a living.

3. A car (or even a driver's license). Mary is determined to get me behind the wheel for the first time in my life. Few share her enthusiasm. Never-drivers are seen as having a slender grasp on reality. Or the way they think is the wrong way to think while driving. They're often literary: Nabokov was driven everywhere by his wife Vera, as I was by my husband. David Sedaris, Gloria Steinem, Studs Terkel (a name like that should have been behind the wheel of a Mack Truck), Alice Munro, Ray Bradbury, J.K. Rowling, Jack Kerouac . . . yes, the man who wrote *On the Road* did not drive. Mary, on the other hand, was an excellent driver. Any troubles she had let go of her behind the wheel, her hands loose as she steered, her dark curls barely stirring as she touched the blinker with a casual flick of her middle finger, turning her head so you'd barely notice to check for traffic. Changing lanes. *Merging.* The wild, improbable freedom of it. As a lifelong passenger and observer of drivers, I greatly admired this ability to appear rakish while driving, the driver and car so intimately acquainted it was almost filthy— who knew what they got up to alone?

4. Another language. As I aged, I steadily assured myself of my general competency by sticking with whatever I was good

at—the best pacing for a happening party, good conversations around books, a fast stride. But with my seventies moving closer, the phrase "Learn new skills!" became a brain loop. I wasn't good at sports that involved balls, but why not try pickleball? Languages weren't a forte either, but maybe I'd brave Spanish classes to talk to my grandson in one of his two languages. It felt safer than a car. At least a grammatical pile-up in Spanish was not going to kill me.

5. Equanimity. "Did something happen to you in your life that makes you nervous?" It was a good question from Mary. I didn't have an answer, except maybe, "being born." I had a dream that baby me was a small red marble, impossible to feed or soothe, although I, the marble, was being driven around in a red convertible.

6. A dog. I had two poodles. Cyrano, a standard, was at the beginning of my marriage and so is remembered with great fondness. Pierre, a miniature, was when the marriage was good but also when it was bad—the dogs shrunk with the marriage—so I have more complicated feelings about him. Since then, I've had no pet of any kind. People I admire say animals are the better part of us, and I sometimes worry I'm missing that part. I think about a cat, and those same people send me pictures of cats that need adoption, which makes us both sad, so I don't mention cats anymore.

7. A husband. The husband I had is still alive, but we don't talk. Our failure is both too big and, by now, too inconsequential. I'm fine with his place on this list, and he would be too.

8. God. Mary has God in her life, and I see the solace, connection, and joy it's brought her, and I'm thankful for that. But my Catholic upbringing got me on the wrong side of God. I don't see that changing.

9. All the goes-with-age stuff. Starting with losing your mind. "Decreased executive functioning along with difficulty word finding and mild inattentiveness," in the words of Nicole Anderson, a scientist I often talk to at Toronto's Baycrest Centre for Aging and Brain Health Innovation. My hippocampus is thinning, and the myelin sheath that surrounds and protects my nerve fibers is wearing down. The wear and tear slows the communication between neurons and also affects my ability to encode new information into my memory. My wise and elastic brain is not as fast and often forgetful. "Don't worry about walking into the kitchen and wondering why you're there," said Anderson. Do worry if you don't know whose kitchen you're in. Don't worry if you can't find your keys (unless they're in the toaster oven). Do worry if you can't remember how to drive. It's fine to search for words, less so to say the wrong words. "That tells smerrible," said a friend recently, and we both paused for a

moment while our brains caught up. "I mean smells terrible," he said. Recovery speed is important.

10. My body next. When I asked my doctor what was going on at sixty-eight, she'd handed me a line drawing of a body entitled "Aging Changes." Organs and bones were neatly drawn inside the body, words and arrows outside. The words "shrivel" and "shrink" appeared more often than I would have liked. The important thing was how many arrows pointed down: muscle mass, blood flow, tidal volume (how much air we breathe). The very few times the arrows pointed up were for body fat and bone breaks. The small fibrillations of panic I had studying the diagram, the merest skips in my heart, were right there under myocardial irritability: "UP ^."

11. Peripheral vision. This, notably, was also a down arrow, with 20 to 30 percent of your visual field gone by seventy, which would explain why my own peripheral vision had become as moody as a teenager in the last year or so—sometimes there, sometimes not. I was not in the big picture, and I didn't see the big picture either.

12. Hearing. Not only what we don't hear—gradually more and more, in my case—but how we hear. "We know that as you age, you speak and listen more slowly," explained

Dr. Björn Herrmann, the research chair on auditory aging at Baycrest. I hadn't been aware of that particular infirmity but added it to the list between my clicking thumb and buckling knee. "We concentrate to understand the words in a sentence and miss the emotion attached to them." Not hearing the prosodic structure or melody of a sentence makes us less likely to understand if the speaker is happy, sad, or angry. Which could explain many conversations with my grown children. *"Mom! We're not arguing with you. We're talking!"*

13. Ease. These gradual physical and mental declines create a lack of ease in the world, a thing you never noticed you had until it's not there anymore. Reading directions fifteen times instead of once. Steeling yourself (just a little) to go outside. Crossing the street. Riding my bike.

14. Time. Only twenty-six more years?

15. A mother. You can feel like a motherless child at sixty-eight. That has no age limit.

16. A father. I walked behind a man who looked just like my dad when he was ninety-two, with a tweed cap and a jaunty step, smart jacket. I passed him and saw that he was my age. My father was a "so far, so good" man. In no way could he be considered a pessimist like Beckett. He taught me to want

what I have, not what I aspire to. This was the secret of his unstoppable and sometimes exasperating optimism: he chose happiness as his guide instead of his goal.

17. A man. People often equate being alone with loneliness, but I love my deepening relationship with solitude. I love my unnegotiated mornings, slowly making pour-over coffee to the quiet of my own thoughts. Making recipes for one. I'm happy with my own version of comfort, which doesn't have to go through the filter of a male human with his own ideas about what that comfort should be. Sure, I sometimes miss that ongoing hopeless annoyance with the other half of the species, whose company I seek precisely because they are not what I am. "I love men. But I hate *coupledom*," my friend Dianne said. "It's a more formal way of being in the world." No, thank you. Being paired up is the last thing I aspire to as I head into the final quarter. My mind is finally free from men; it expands into its own constellated universe.

Be careful what you don't want. It has a way of finding you.

seven

OLD FRIEND, PART 1

THIS IS HOW IT BEGAN.

The subject line of the email at 8:28 a.m. on a Thursday in February was "Old Friend." The email itself was brief: *Good to see that you've done well. Remember the old days. D.*

D was my first love, and the first boy I had sex with, when I was seventeen. He broke up with me when he left our small town to go to university. I didn't go around thinking about him in the decades that followed—he was in the far past—but I hadn't forgotten him either. He was a belowground memory.

I saw D for the first time across the schoolyard when I was fourteen and he was fifteen. I don't recall looking away, or being self-conscious that I didn't look away, when my gaze landed on him sitting cross-legged on the ground, his back against a brick wall. "He belonged still to himself at fifteen/ waiting for the later years to reach him," Michael Ondaatje wrote in his poem "Wanderer" and maybe that's what I saw. A boy who belonged to no one else. Or was it that his head was bent over a book, and I loved reading more than anything at fourteen, so it was my own blooming self that drew me to him? Something new and separate began at that moment too—a second birth, out of my family at home and into a family of friends, almost as secret as reading, and not to be shared with the adults. That might have been some of what went on that day in the schoolyard.

We hadn't spoken to each other for more than fifty years, so this email was an unexpected start to an otherwise standard-issue sunless February morning. I appreciated the lack of a question mark in the second sentence. Some questions are better without them. I immediately forwarded his email to Meryl, who would remember D from Grimsby. She immediately called me.

"Don't you think it sounds so paternalistic?" I asked. Meryl and I usually spoke at night, beginning our calls with "Just a minute," as we each settled into our own beds, under the covers, half a province apart. We were always cold. But this call was an emergency, so we were in our kitchens, in the morning. "*Oh*," I imitated a pompous manvoice. "*You've* done well for *your*self."

I was certain Meryl would agree with me. On a trip back to our hometown several years earlier, I had been reminiscing about D as we climbed the Niagara Escarpment—"I think I necked with him right over there," I'd said, looking fondly at a bright clump of birch trees—when Meryl interrupted me. "I couldn't figure out what you were doing with him. He was full of himself and not very nice to you." "Pardon?" I'd never thought of myself as a wild romantic, but had I wildly romanticized my first love? And given who I eventually married, had I been repeating the same relationship ever since?

I fully expected Meryl to scoff along with me. Instead, she took his side.

"'You've done well' is what he wrote," Meryl corrected and disappointed me at the same time. "It seems like a simple statement of fact to me. You *have* done well." She'd read the email to her husband to get a man's opinion.

"What'd he say?"

"Take it at face value."

Before she hung up, Meryl told me about a study that said 70 percent of people who reconnect with their first loves end up marrying them. (That study was from 1993, a more innocent time. Little more than a decade later, casual connections on the internet had ushered in the era of noncommittal romance: by then, people had affairs with their former lovers, but only 5 percent ended up marrying.) I did my own online scan and discovered that the first-love redo was so common it was practically an industry. Suddenly D's reappearance in my life seemed nostalgic, rootsy, even conservative. Certainly not specific and singular, which was how I had been imagining myself. Digital modernity has made it vastly easier to connect with former loves. Whether doing so is wise is less clear, especially at a time of life when the upheaval of new love can feel more like ruin than romance. My days were full with children, grandchildren, friends, writing. Why squeeze out any of that steady happiness to make space for something unknown and precarious?

I waited three days to reply to D, perhaps the only sensible thing I did in all that came next. At noon on the following Sunday, I wrote:

Hey. For sure I remember the old days. How are you? The last I knew about you, you were on your way to becoming a doctor.

Yes, I went to medical school and then trained in psychiatry, but that is now thankfully winding down.

At first the emails were cool, mildly interested, catching up on details. The day of the initial back-and-forth, after the three-day pause, was my birthday and Laura had invited Mary and me to her place for dinner. When we finished eating, I opened a pretty pair of dangly earrings from Mary and then the first of Laura's presents: a blue plastic disc, about the size of my hand.

"I almost bought myself one of these the other day." I held it toward the light. I was really pleased. "You read my mind. Thank you, Laura."

"Oh, my God, *Mom*!" Mary, sitting across from me with her dark curls tied back, had covered her face with her hands. "Why would you need a diva cup?"

"Diva cup?" Laura and I said simultaneously.

I grabbed a jar of mustard from Laura's fridge and fitted the plastic over the lid. "It's a jar opener!"

After the birthday cake, which was a small, heart-shaped tart, like the ones Mom used to make me because my birthday was so close to Valentine's Day, I read Laura and Mary the first line of the first email from D. Laura agreed with me.

"He could have said, 'Congratulations on your brilliant career,' or something more like that. Less patriarchal."

"Right?" I knew I'd been right. "A little pat on the head."

"Let me see the emails." Mary reached her hand across the table with the weary authority of adult children around anything their parents do online and then bent over my phone. "Oh, my God, Mom! You sound like a jilted teenager, like you broke up two days ago instead of fifty years ago. Just relax, why don't you? Write like a person."

When I got into bed later that night, after a walk home through a vitalizing winter rain, I began what would become a true correspondence with D, with who we were, young, at seventeen, and who we were becoming, old, near seventy. Each email inhabited time and space in a mysterious new dimension, easy to write in but hard to follow linearly. There was a luxuriousness to time, and I had become adrift in it. "I'm speeded up, so time is slowed down," was how D put it. Without knowing it, I was entering the same place I'd been in with him when I was a girl. I couldn't tell you who I was at twenty-six or forty-four or fifty-eight, but seventeen was the time I felt most like myself. I was keen to know that Cathrin again.

I wrote that I wasn't expecting him to be a psychiatrist (this secretly fascinated me, both the profession and him choosing it) and asked him where he lived now. We discovered that we had lived in the same city for forty-five years, often within a few blocks of each other, sometimes even in neighboring houses on the same street, though not simultaneously. Perhaps we'd been affecting each other without knowing it, he wrote one night. Even now we lived just a forty-minute walk apart. He showed me how to fly from his house to my house on Google Maps.

And then we'd swing back in time to Grimsby and our past there, the past that made us quickly and easily comfortable with each other, and more open than we might otherwise have been. We shared details about our friends from when we were teenagers. It was 1968 to 1974, when eight or ten of us hung out in the park in the center of town and on the steps of the post office—long-haired, peasant-dressed, acid-dropping teenage hippies. We read Sartre's *Nausea* and Dostoyevsky's *Notes from Underground*. We sucked on sugar cubes dipped in tea, starving artists that we were, before we went home for meatloaf and mashed potatoes with our moms and dads. We struggled and failed to be uninhibited. We were sweet and innocent, the last things we imagined we were. We were good friends too, the boys and the girls, although none of us would have put it that way to each other. Being in the same place at the same time, smoking and not saying much, was how our friendship was expressed.

Our town wasn't innocent. D wanted me to understand this. It was the subversive 1960s, and even in a place like Grimsby, Ontario, population eight thousand, we were surrounded by transgression, gangs of bikers taking over the main street, parents going wild (not mine). I faintly remembered the feral families of siblings that seemed to have no visible parents.

I'm telling you it wasn't no Sleepytown. We were teen spies, those parents didn't know how much we saw . . . Hey, what about Arlene?

My grudge against Arlene, whom D had a crush on part of the time he was with me, was suddenly as fresh as cut grass. Obviously, D had never read the advice of Kingsley Amis, as reported by his son, Martin: "In conversations with women, never even mention another woman's name—unless it is to report her (very painful) death."

"It's ridiculous." I was on the phone with Ellen this time. "I am not going to become unhinged from the life I'm living, which is exactly the life I want." I made the verbal equivalent of rolling my eyes. "I don't even know him, for one thing."

The silence was so complete, I thought the line had gone dead.

"Hello, hello. Are you there?"

"I'm here." Ellen's voice was stern, and I thought she was going to say, "You're too old for this," but she surprised me the same way Meryl had. "I don't know why you're being glib about something that's obviously important. Someone you had a deep connection with is writing to you about that connection. This is not something to laugh off or be sarcastic about. Plus you sound completely rattled."

"I'm not rattled at all." I didn't know if it was Tuesday or Friday.

"Yes, you are. I've never heard you so rattled." Ellen had her own D, same first name. They'd also met when she was fourteen, he fifteen, and were on and off again until she was twenty-one. Her D became a doctor too. The coincidences were baffling, with the difference that Ellen and her D had stayed in touch with letters and emails, even meeting once or twice. Now they talked every week on Zoom, he in Winnipeg, she in Toronto, a deep and meaningful relationship for both.

Once again, using my old-age brain elasticity, my both-sides wisdom, I waited for several days before I reported to D that Arlene had gone *off the rails* and I hadn't heard anything about her for a long time. It was when he replied immediately with *I'm glad you wrote back* that I took a small but decisive tumble in his direction.

Quickly, I knew much more about D than I had when we were young. You understand as much as you ever will at seventeen. But things like where you were born and what your father's job was tend not to come up. D's father had spent his war, from age twenty to twenty-five, in a British POW camp in Poland. His family moved from Devon, England, to Northern Ontario when D was a kid, so his outsider status in the schoolyard would have been part of what turned my head. I found out that his mother left her husband when she was fifty to merge households with a new man. But the important thing about this piece of information was that it was the first time the word "love" was put on the page between us.

It was a bit of a scandal. My mom seemed to have found love for the first time. For me, it was like a version of Hamlet.

And then, closing the time warp:

Without realizing it, I was telling you a story about older people finding love. Or trying to find some way to pick up our story where it was left off when we were 17.

Maybe he'd secretly felt the same way I did that time in the schoolyard? It was an astonishing thought. I'd just heard a podcast of Irish author Sebastian Barry describing the sighting of his own first love, when he was fifteen and she thirteen, as "cataclysmic radiance." I'm the same age as Barry and often feel like we're going through the same thing at the same time. He writes incandescently about all love, but when it's about men and women, the heat visibly radiates off the page.

I think I had cataclysmic radiance the first time I saw you.

I'm sorry. I don't remember seeing you in the schoolyard.

This would become a typical response to my memories of us at fifteen or seventeen. He remembered much less than I did. Not about all things, or even most things. He remembered the color of the frozen lake in 1967, *the shades of gray in all directions,* the black branches with red berries that arched over it. He remembered kissing Nancy Wilson's neck, and the first time he saw a certain kid named Al.

Hope that isn't too insulting, but it was my first day at a new school and I was drawn to the cast on his arm with a sticker saying "Bring them Back Alive."

He took my first memory of him with his book in the schoolyard seriously, though. It showed where our own lives were going: books, ideas, adventure, love. We were both retired, but I wrote and he was a practicing *psychiatrist of thought,* as he described it, and spent about five hours a day reading French philosophers from the mid-twentieth century—Diderot, Deleuze, Sartre, Camus. I'd often wake up to an email about Hegelian dichotomies (D disapproved of my tasky-lists and was trying to reform how I thought of them) or Nietzsche's Eternal Return, which perhaps we were in together, seventy going on seventeen.

To live as if this moment is eternal rather than part of a chronology. So that obviously we would have to return to each other.

Maybe it was the terror of having to revisit Hegel—I'd studied Hegelian systems of thought in my second year at university, and the experience struck me mute for two semesters. Or maybe it was my 7 a.m. swoon over our eternal return. But I was the one who put sex on the page.

Not knowing anything. Except how good it felt. I'm very happy that was my first experience of sex, that you were. It was big. Important.

My parents reliably went out on weekends when we were teenagers. Meryl called it "the era of the Saturday nights," when everyone would pile into my house and (some, not Meryl) would hive off into bedrooms, then join back up in the living room for a communal smoke. Except my mom and dad were in their own eternal return, always coming home too soon. They'd walk through the side door as people were fleeing over the fence in the backyard.

Our encounters have been neatly edited into "and then I somehow escaped," D wrote.

But we were creating something between us back then. We both believed that fifty years later. I think two people can make a force field, and that's the force of the universe right there in the space between you. If you're lucky, you give yourself over to a thing you can't fully understand. You connect with it, and then you connect with everything else all at once. Having that with D made me the lucky one. To have carried that first connection through the rest of love that came. It was different for him.

We had a connection but then it was lost so it feels for me like something missed in both senses of the word. But I've been wondering about you all these years. Wondering if you'd say, "you've got a lot of nerve to say you are my friend."

I replied quickly. *You did hurt me when I was 18. A mortal blow.* I paused and added. *Then I went on to hurt and love other people, of course.*

"I was surprised how painful the memory of his rejection was, so many years later." I'd managed to drag myself out of my bed—I was spending a lot of time there, staring into the middle distance—to join Ellen and Sally for a walk at Cherry Beach in the east end of the city. "I've tucked that pain away for five decades. It feels dangerous to open myself up to it again."

Behind us was the same rough winter lake that D and I had walked along in Grimsby, just on the other side. "Stand still." I took Ellen by the arm and aimed my phone. Not her favorite thing, being touched, but I wanted D to see me as I was in the present, old, lined, and cheery, against a familiar place from our past. Then and now. Ellen and I posed in our huge coats and eccentric hats, grimace-smiling as the wet wind whipped our faces. I flipped the selfie to D.

"Rugged," he wrote back. I resolved to send him a better picture at the earliest opportunity.

"Are you going to spend our entire walk on your phone?" Ellen was irked.

"Pardon?" I put my phone in my pocket.

"You're acting like a scared rabbit." This was a bit much, even for Ellen's new speak-only-the-truth persona, which I was still getting used to. I saw myself as more of a bold hare, leaping forward after considered pauses.

"Stop writing and meet, for God's sake." Ellen threw a stick into the lake for Sally, who declined to fetch it. Sally wasn't really a dog. She was a human in dog disguise. "It's time to get off the page."

eight

ON THE ROAD, PART 2:
THE SECRET PASSAGEWAY

"HOW ABOUT WE PULL OFF in Fruitland, to see the orchards?" This was an off-plan idea from Laura, in the driver's seat.

"There's no fruit in Fruitland," I said, waving away the exit. Normally, on a car trip, I'd be keeping my mouth shut in the back, since I don't drive and am not renowned for my navigation skills. But this trip was my idea, so Ann, who'd come from Vancouver, took the back seat and I rode up front. I was heady with power.

"Let's just keep going until we get there."

We were on our way to Grimsby. A man named Tim (yes, *another* Tim, not to be confused with my brother Tim or Tim the Jungian) had been in touch to say he'd read something I'd written about my childhood and recognized the house I'd grown up in as the house where he now lived with his wife and two sons. "If you would ever like to visit, you'd be very welcome."

It wasn't a minor thing, to come home. There was the recently reopened past in Grimsby with D. But mostly it was the house. It compelled me: from the moment I read the email I felt spellbound to go. I'm not the only one to get this way about a house. Margaret Atwood has written about long-lived-in houses as repositories for memory since *Surfacing* in 1972. Or how Deborah Levy put it in *Real Estate*, the third book of her ongoing autobiography: the places "we live in as children live in us as adults." It had been fifty years since I'd been through its doors, but I knew this house better than any other place. I knew the view out every window—lawns and driveways, mostly. I knew where the baseboards warped; I'd dusted them enough. The secrets my mother kept in the deep built-in drawers of her bedroom dresser—the pink disc of birth control pills, the paper-bag-covered *Joy of Sex*—were mine to ransack and then carefully put back.

My parents paid $16,000 for the one-and-a-half-story wood-frame in 1962. Like most of the houses on the street, it had been built by Gordon Schaefer who lived next door with his wife. We called him Mr. Schaefer, and he seemed old to us kids, but he'd have been younger than I am now. In the 1920s, he'd had a vision for a street with a treed boulevard and workable houses for working families, and he built it. This was before the cookie-cutter developments of the 1950s, so each house on Nelles Boulevard looked different on the outside—ours featured a barn roof, for example. The insides had modern built-in cupboards (Mr. Schaefer's trademark), deep walk-in closets, and central-hall layouts: living/dining rooms to the left, den to the right, kitchen in back, three bedrooms, two bathrooms, one bathtub—and in our house, seven people. There would have been a lot going on, Mom at the center. When we moved in, she was forty, the middle age of adulthood; I was seven, the middle age of childhood. We both came into ourselves there, or one version of it.

When I dreamed of a house it was almost always this house, and when I dreamed of my mother it was almost always in this house, grinning at me in the kitchen or her bedroom or the cement-floored basement. Not frail and timid old Mom, twisting Kleenex in her hands, the ailing mother I felt guilty about—not when she was alive but relentlessly from the moment she was no longer there for me to help. And not the mother I was afraid of becoming in my own journey to old age—and what was to prevent it, after all? My ten thousand steps a day, my devastatingly sensible footwear, my silken tofu?

No. I had come home to find my ready, undaunted mother, the woman who ran an invisible empire raising five children in this house on Nelles Boulevard. I didn't know the connection between who she was here, in her prime, and who she became thirty years later. But maybe the house did.

"Pull off in Fruitland and all you'll see are orchards paved over with condominiums," I said, underlining my no-detour position. This was true. Highway 8, once the scenic route from Hamilton to St. Catharines, lined with sumptuous orchards of peach and cherry trees, had mostly been turned into a commuter corridor to Toronto. So instead, we drove to Grimsby on the Queen Elizabeth Highway (QEW) as it passed through the outskirts of towns like the spurned Fruitland. The buildings on either side of the QEW were an aggressively ugly staccato of office blocks with names like VersaCold Logistic Services or Automation Palletizing and Food Material Handling. But just to the south were the thrillingly crashing waves of Lake Ontario.

"It's north," Laura said. "People always get that confused. "When you're in Grimsby, the lake is north and the Niagara Escarpment is south. It's the opposite of Toronto, basically." We were on the underside of the Great Lake now, like in an upside-down fairy tale where nothing is quite the same.

"I'd like to see Grimsby High," said Ann, another off-plan idea, and this time I didn't object. We stepped out of the black Subaru into the oppressive August heat and walked up the steps of the secondary school that Ann and Laura had graduated from, and that I had dropped out of after eleventh grade in a barely-thought-through protest of organized education. Not something I talked about.

"This is *exactly* the same," said Ann as we peered through the locked doors at the gleaming brown- and orange-tiled 1970s decor.

We posed for a group selfie on the school steps, and Ann stood in the back because she didn't like how her new black shift was hanging. "Get out from behind me, Ann." I gave her a small shove. Our relationship had developed a physical component in middle age. She was too little to shove when we were kids, me being eight years older. But lately she'd started poking me with her index finger as she talked, my arm if we were walking and my leg if we were sitting. *Poke, poke.* Sometimes I would grab her finger and hold it, or I'd take her whole hand and squeeze it hard. "Don't poke me!" I considered carrying a straight pin to jab her with, an Ellen suggestion, but had not. So far.

"Would you like me to take your picture?" A smiling woman came up to us as we shoved around on the steps of the high school.

"We all went to school here," Laura said.

"I dropped out." Apparently I'd decided to start saying this out loud to strangers.

"This is to be torn down," the friendly woman told us, for a new regional superschool, and we got going about the destruction of precious farmland along the Niagara Peninsula and the tree-bulldozing enthusiasts of the Grimsby town council.

When I posted our photo on Instagram, I immediately received a comment from our nephew Conor in Toronto: "Hope you all walked with caution."

I was wondering if he'd sensed the shoving from the look on my face, but then I noticed the sign behind our heads, above the double-doored entrance: *Grimsby Secondary School: Please follow posted traffic signs & walk with caution. Be safe!*

"Oh, my God, we're eight minutes early."

I jerked my hand back from the doorbell I was about to ring when I noticed the numbers on my Apple Watch said 11:52 a.m. I held a bouquet of yellow flowers bought when we'd stopped at a local florist half an hour earlier, giving us time to arrive at our childhood home at precisely 12 p.m. My sisters and I were eccentrically punctual, and sometimes accidentally arrived ahead of schedule. I yanked them down the porch steps we had just walked up.

"Let go," said Ann, shaking me off. Of the three sisters, she was the least inclined to panic.

"We'll walk around the block for eight minutes," Laura said reassuringly, backing down the stairs with me. We were in the middle of our disorderly retreat when the door swung open.

"It's the Bradbury sisters!" Our host had been waiting at the door like our parents would have been. Our mother believed in being a good wife, a job that kept her hopping mad 90 percent of the time. She would have spent the morning vacuuming and scrubbing in a building fury. She'd rise to the occasion of our arrival, though. She loved an occasion. She'd have sewn us new outfits to greet our old selves, poking us with pins—*there's the poking*—as we turned and turned on the kitchen table. When the doorbell rang, we'd be dressed to the nines at noon on a Saturday while we nursed our bruises behind her.

Tim had no pretense. He was medium-sized, with an open stance and a big smile on his round face; a jolly, Dickensian man. He immediately relaxed us. "Come in, come in." He ushered us over the threshold and into the front hall, or what used to be the front hall. Instead, we were at the entrance of a white room with some kind of wire fence to the left that I was trying to make sense of until I realized it was a makeshift barrier for the taffy-colored dog that was barking its head off at us.

"Odin's our new puppy." Tim nodded to the smaller of two boys, who picked up yappy Odin. Then he introduced Elliot, who looked to be about the same age as me when I moved here, seven or so, and Aiden, maybe twelve, tall and thin, with hair to his shoulders and a quiet seriousness in contrast to his father's noisy joy.

"Now, which of you is Cathrin?" Tim looked from sister to sister.

"She is." Laura pointed to me. "I'm Laura, the oldest, and this is Ann, the youngest."

I handed Tim the yellow flowers, and he put them unceremoniously on the kitchen island behind him. *Kitchen island,* what the bloody hell? I struggled to follow the greetings and introductions. This wasn't anything like looking into our untouched high school. There was nothing to hold on to, in this blown-out, open-concept, all-white space with a kitchen island. The only thing I knew with unpleasant clarity was that Mom would not be found here, and neither would I.

"This is exactly what I would have done," Laura was saying pleasantly to Tim. "Opened the whole thing up."

Did Mom say you could do this? I was thinking, I hoped not saying, as my mind filled in the linoleum hallway with a phone at the end and rooms on either side. Time was becoming unbound, like that movie trope when the pages of a book go flying. What was the order of the story? I managed to get out, "I see you kept the fireplace."

The tour of the main floor consisted of standing still and looking around us because there were no walls to hinder the view. "So much light!" Laura was still going on. She'd lived here the shortest time before she left for university, so was fully in the present with the tour and the family. Sure, sure, nice light. But the lack of rooms made everything seem smaller. Until we got to the basement, where time whooshed open again. The rec room with the 1960s-style bar—the room where I'd had sex for the first time with D on a low single bed—was mostly the same. The cement-floored laundry room was intact too. Ann opened the latch to the root cellar, where our mother's preserves had been kept—and we three sisters all leaned in to breathe the damp-earth smell, like a secret rich thought. "It smells *exactly* the same," said Ann.

It was when we headed for the second floor that the house—my house—settled into place, like one of those shuddering buildings in Harry Potter that finally lets you in. Mom moved our bedrooms around so often you never knew where you'd land, but we all coveted the little room at the top of the stairs, now Elliot's, because it was too small to share and offered the rare gift of privacy. Elliot jumped onto the built-in bed, claiming it, and a cruise-ship of stuffed animals bounced high in the air with him. Next was the big bedroom with a smaller annex, always shared by at least two of us, now all Aiden's. Under the window in the main bedroom was his horticultural station with its plants and heat lamps. Laura Appleseed gave Aiden a seed packet she'd been carrying around from the flower store. They got deep into the tomato plants while Ann and I stood in the annex.

Which was when little Elliot looked up at his father, as if for permission. His father nodded, and Elliot pushed a button or lever I couldn't see. The bookshelf against the wall suddenly swung open. Elliot had been silent for the whole tour, and he remained so as he performed a magician's sweep of his hand: *Ta-da!*

"Is that a secret passageway?" I said, peering into what looked like a dark tunnel, about three feet high.

Elliot nodded.

"Where does it go?" Ann asked. She was as surprised as I was.

"To our bedroom," said Tim. Meaning to my mom and dad's bedroom.

"So you built this passageway?" I was assembling the facts.

"No," he said. "It was always here. I just added the entryway."

Elliot gestured for me to go in. Odin, his little dog, barked. I looked from the puppy to Elliot to Tim to Ann, everyone's faces expectant, uncertain, waiting. *Walk with caution,* the sign at the high school had warned. My compulsion to see this house had brought me to the entrance of a secret passageway, and that was something. Where would it take me if I went in? From myself at sixty-eight—becoming someone I wasn't sure I knew—to the child version of me, who had become someone new in this house, sixty years ago? As a journey from here to there, this one felt like the trickiest.

I quickly understood, however, that if I got on my hands and knees, ass in the air for all to see, and crawled to my parents' former bedroom, the only thing that would happen would be a diminishment of my dignity. And I didn't quite have the courage to face that. It might have been the easier choice, though. Because not going through the secret passageway would keep Mom waiting for me at the other end.

Directly from Grimsby, we three sisters headed north to Laura's off-grid cabin, located on a profoundly quiet lake (no power hum or motorboats) in the Haliburton Highlands. There we met up with Ann's two daughters, on their own significant trip. Keogh, twenty-one, was driving across the country, a rite of passage for Canadians, to take her younger sister, Claire, from Vancouver to Concordia University in Montreal. Claire, eighteen, was leaving home, after growing up in a house not unlike the one we had just visited in Grimsby: welcoming, cared for, cheerful. Their long drive in Ann's orange Suzuki, through the choking wildfires of a burning British Columbia, was a daring and brave adventure, and we heard the story as the girls plunged in and out of the rippled lake, cooling their bodies and their souls under the barely clouded sky. Let's put Mary on the dock too, because she often was. She'd lead the cannonball charge into the water.

"What would it have cost to get a four-step ladder?" I asked Laura, not for the first time, because her three-step ladder from the dock got me only as deep as my thighs, defeating the purpose of the old-woman-ease-in entry.

"Another fifty dollars!" she called out from where she was doing the crawl with her head above the water, the same way she had since she was a girl. Later, settled with our splay of towels, hats, sunscreen, books, drinks, snacks, coolers, folding chairs, and a blue umbrella for the aunts—it looked like we'd packed for a month-long excursion instead of the two-minute walk down to the water from the cabin—I told my daughter and nieces about Ann and me standing at the portal to the secret passageway to our own mother.

"Get *out*!" Claire almost rolled off the dock. "Oh, my God, Mom," said Mary, "remember how I used to read in the cubbyhole in the basement and pretend it had an elevator to your bedroom closet upstairs?"

I didn't, but this was a very satisfying reaction. The girls had read dozens of books featuring secret passageways—a lot I'd never heard of and the classics too, like *Coraline*, where the Other Mother on the other side of the wall sews buttons over children's eyes and eats their souls for breakfast.

"I have negative mother complex," said Ann from her lounger. Our daughters had gone for a paddle and were out of earshot, or else we might not have gotten onto the subject of mothers. You don't want to give your kids an opening to take a shot at you for your own failures.

"Who doesn't?" Laura said from her chair with her hat over her face.

"I don't know what you two are talking about." I rolled onto my stomach on the dock and closed my eyes. I knew what a mother complex was. I just didn't want to have anything to do with it, even as I was in its grips.

"Mom had me accidentally, at thirty-nine, so she had to do it all over again," said Ann. "But she was out of reserves. She wanted her life back."

Laura corroborated Ann's version because she had become the substitute mother—"Ann called *me* Mama"—and spent much of her teen years looking after not only Ann but all four of her younger siblings.

"Mom absent?" I propped myself up on my elbows, amazed out of my sun stupor. "She was *never* not there!" Every sibling in every family has different parents, maybe especially in a sibling family that has a fifteen-year span like ours. When Mom was gone, her version of me was gone too, but not my version of her. My internal mother was layered, durable, and deeply present. The way we experience a parent, never enough love or always too much, doesn't stop after they die. Certainly, there were three moms floating around on the dock that afternoon.

As dusk came down, we exhausted the subjects of passageways and mothers and began to prepare a dinner of fresh corn, tomatoes, and peaches bought on our way out of Grimsby, in Fruitland. "I told you there was fruit in Fruitland," said Laura.

It was a good day with five sisters, and it ended around the campfire, flames dancing on our faces and darkness pressing against our backs as we read aloud from Claire's copy of *Heidi*, the story of a motherless girl with her own journey home to make.

"I need to go into your crawl space," I told my friend Tecca, who'd recently bought a house with an underground passage to get to her electrical panels. Tecca raised an eyebrow, but quickly opened a large wooden trap door under the rug on the kitchen floor, no questions asked. "You'll want these knee-pads," she said, which I declined and immediately regretted as my knees connected with the bracingly hard cement floor. But the space itself was open and clean, a place for metal panels and extension cords, not magic and time travel.

"That crawl space was always there." My pragmatic brother David had been a venturesome boy when we swapped bedrooms at Nelles Boulevard and had found what started as a cubbyhole in my parent's walk-in closet, hidden by my father's work suits. But beyond the boxes of Christmas decorations, if you dared—as I did not—the cubbyhole kept going along the front of the house. "It was roomy and clean," David told me, disappointingly. "Though also secret," I'd pressed him. "Sort of forbidden?"

As I grappled with the (I'll grant possibly) unhinged idea that I'd missed the opportunity to find my mother at the end of the passageway, I wondered less about who I'd be and more about which mother she would have been. Surely the young and vital woman who raised me here, the indominable mother I'd gone home to find. Except she was never that, of course. Mothers only seem undefeated to their children.

My mother had her own dreams of being a writer when she was young, but she came of age during wartime, was married by twenty-one, and seemed middle-aged with four children by thirty. Maybe she'd glimpsed a chance at an inward life before she became pregnant for the fifth time, or maybe just a job that paid money. When something you long for gets thwarted, a fear settles into you, of the risks you couldn't take. And then it comes back the next time you have to risk everything, the way getting old grabs hold of you, with its bottomless stream of fear and worry. I thought about how I'd have put that into a question for Mom, if I'd found her at the end of the secret passageway.

"I would ask if she loved me," said Ann.

"I used to stand outside Mom's bedroom door and listen to her sing to you as she rocked you in the white chair that had always been there," I said to my sister. "It made me understand that she had sung to all her babies like that, in that white chair. Watching you being loved made me know that I was loved too."

Ellen and I often talked about missing our mothers. We liked to put them up in heaven. Ellen was a lapsed Catholic too, and heaven was coming up a lot. "The birds will be singing where they are, and it will always smell great," I said. "You know, heavenly."

"That could get old fast," said Ellen. Her idea was strolling around in the clouds trading wisecracks with her dad. "And when I find my mother," she said, "we'll talk about everything I wish we had when she was alive." It's one of those things that becomes vivid in the back quarter of life, if you had a good mother—the conversations you might have had.

As I thought about the secret passageway, I began to realize that it wasn't my young mother I wanted to get to but my old one. Not to hear what she could tell me, but to say what I wish I'd said to her when she was alive: "It's okay, Mom. Don't be scared. I'm here."

When we were at the door about to leave our childhood home, Tim the owner produced a leather binder with a two-page typewritten history of the house. It had a brief description of each owner—my parents were fifth, Tim and his family seventh. The owners between us, who had put together the binder, wrote, "This home holds many happy memories for all our family. Best wishes from both Barry and me, Georgina."

Next, Tim showed us a framed photograph of 3 Nelles Boulevard, taken in 1925. "But it's the only house on the street," I said. It was the only house around, in fact, with the broad horizon of the Great Lake to the north, and the somber sky above. The rest of the streets didn't exist yet.

"Number 3 was the first house Mr. Schaefer built," Tim said. The picture had been taken from the point of the Niagara Escarpment, which sloped up at the end of our street. As a kid, I'd climbed to that same point to find my house crowded in among the other houses below, shouting, "There it is! There's mine!" All the kids did the same, finding their houses below. Locating ourselves. We didn't know how lucky we were: to have a house, to see it, to go home to it. I looked at the photograph Tim handed me for as long as I could. It seemed to be saying something too simple to see. Before we said goodbye, I took a picture of the picture, and I often look at it, trying to figure something out.

On another hot August day, after the visit to Grimsby, I bought a plastic wading pool for my grandson. The inflatable pool was a moderate success—he didn't go in, only splashed from outside. But the box the pool came in was another story. It featured a bright photograph of a family, two kids and a mom, everybody in the pool. My grandson could not stop looking at this picture. He sat on the chair beside the actual pool and stared at the photograph of the pool for a long time. It seemed to me, watching him, that he was realizing it wasn't just his pool but this other family's pool too. And that the happiness this pool brought to families, not just his own, was the essence of its poolness, separate from any of us.

The house on Nelles Boulevard is the house I dream of, and also a dream house. Mom had done that. She'd given us the dream of a happy home, or as close to it as she could get. Seven families came and went, and the house held all their memories, which gave it a memory too. The past and present were pressed together inside its walls (give or take a few), all happening at once. It had stood there alone one hundred years ago, and it would likely still be there for a hundred more, if the bulldozers didn't get to it sooner.

nine

OLD FRIEND, PART 2

THIS IS HOW IT ENDED.

I came home on a clear and cold March afternoon, walked directly to the kitchen with my bulky black winter coat still zipped, and grabbed a cold bottle of twist-top Gavi from the fridge. *Glug glug glug* was the sound the wine made, that's how hard my pour was. I'd just lifted it to my mouth, the glass brimming like a lake after an epic spring thaw, when Maria walked in on me and my pursed lips.

"You look like you need that," she said.

"I do." It was 3 p.m. Maria smiled neutrally, open to what might come.

Maria was twenty-five. When she wasn't driving a giant black SUV on the Inuvik–Tuktoyaktuk Highway, doing research for her PhD—"They call me Tiny because you can hardly see me behind the wheel"—she rented a light-filled room on the second floor of my house. She was my fifth border since my divorce eight years earlier—a plan I came up with partly to help with the triple-sized mortgage I acquired after buying out my husband, and partly because the sounds in the night made my squat stucco house with its four sides of windows feel as vulnerable as a bird on the road. It hadn't helped that I'd been broken into twice; one thief climbed through the dining room window as I sat at the table. I needed a good night's sleep, a problem having other people in the house solved instantly. The less expected pleasure was how each of the women, students who came from all over to live with me for a year or three, made the world smaller and more personal.

"My first boyfriend from when I was a girl emailed me a month ago," I said.

Maria crossed her arms and leaned against the fridge. She was a willow of a woman, thin and bendy. She nodded solemnly for me to continue my story. I took two more glugs of wine.

"We emailed back and forth for a few weeks, and just now we met for the first time in fifty years." I looked up woefully from my glass. "It didn't go so well."

Maria remained quiet as I told her more of the story, my coat still zipped. I could see she was considering whether to say more. She was exceptionally well mannered.

"If I may suggest a couple of things you might have done differently?"

"Please do," I said, wagging the bottle in her general direction. "Wine?"

"No, I'm okay." She put the kettle on for tea. A spring robin, harbinger of better days, hopped outside on the grass, head cocked like he was listening to our conversation, as robins do.

"Poor thing," said Maria. "The next polar vortex is going to wipe him out."

"Robins get by," I said. They were the size of small cats, for one thing. "He'll be fine."

"The first thing I'd say," Maria began, "is never email back and forth for more than a few days before you meet."

"Really?" I felt like Moses getting the lowdown from God on how to live right. I almost reached my arms out to accept the thunderous tablet of her truth: *Thou shalt not email potential date for more than three days before meeting.*

"Yes, really." The kettle whistled, and she turned her back on me briefly to pour a cup of tea before facing me again, the mug steaming between her hands. "You get intimate online, and then if you meet and there isn't a connection, it's painful for at least one of you, or maybe both. Expectations and hopes build up." Maria had met her current guy online, and they both understood rules like this—rules I would later broadcast to everyone I knew, like the hottest breaking news.

"No kidding, just a few days?" said my sister Ann. "Scams, nutjobs, you have to be careful of those kinds of things at this age, or that's the usual advice. I know women who email for six months before they agree to meet a man."

"Big mistake," I said. "Big, big, big mistake."

Will you be outside of Future Bakery or inside? I wrote as I zipped myself into my bulky black coat.

I put on my sunglasses and walked, head down, the three blocks to where we'd agreed to meet, outside. I pictured D. as I walked. Older, of course, but still an outsider, I knew that from his emails. Radical in a meaningful way because he'd lived his whole life according to his values, tending to the sickest of the sick, never taking more than he needed, keeping his footprint small and his spending modest. A committed ground traveler. I was keen to walk with him, the way he'd loped beside me when we were young, me walking on air—not just an emotion but a physical sensation of being about a foot off the ground. He'd be leaning against a wall on the corner where we'd agreed to meet. I imagined his head in a book. No, come on, get a grip—his head in his phone. I'd stand in front of him, and he'd look up slowly, interested but distanced, the same way he had at fifteen.

I was startled out of myself by an iron-haired man calling to me from across the street. "You look exactly the same!" The impossibility of this statement was immediately apparent because to look at him was to see how old I had become.

("The only thing harder than seeing yourself grow old is seeing the people you've loved grow old," wrote Sigrid Nunez in *What Are You Going Through*.) As surprising as D's age was his unexpected enthusiasm. His hands seemed to be clutched to his heart as I stood at the red light. When I crossed at the green, he embraced me in a hug for some time. Then he asked if he could lift me up into the air.

"I don't think so, no."

He put his arm around me instead, and we headed south, on foot.

"I'm a little uncomfortable with your arm around me," I said after half a block.

He removed his arm from my shoulder and instead took my hand in both of his and pulled me close to him. Then he kissed me, the first of many, just a light brush on the lips, but a kiss all the same.

"For me, a kiss is pretty intimate," I said, on one of our pauses on a park bench. I had no idea where I was. It was cold, I knew that much, but I didn't feel it. It must've been the bulky black coat.

"I'm sorry. I'll stop." Instead, he kissed me again. "Look at you!" He walked around me, looking at me. He stroked my arm and back through my coat. It was difficult to reshape my mouth from the eerie grin it had set into.

—

"May I tell you the second mistake you made?" Maria said, back in the kitchen. I steadied myself against the counter to take in her next lesson from the top of the online-dating mountain.

"Please do."

"The etiquette is that before people meet on their first date, they agree how they'll behave. So, for example, before I met my boyfriend, he asked me how we should greet each other. If I would like to shake hands or hug or kiss, or not make any physical contact at all. This is very common now."

"You can't be serious." I was awestruck.

"It saves you from a lot of discomfort in the first meeting. You know what's going to happen, at least in the first half hour or so."

D and I walked for three hours, I knew that much because it was three thirty in my kitchen, and I'd met D at noon. As we walked and talked I began to see the outlines of the boy in his still wavy hair and his strong hands. Something in the expression of his face was remembered, inquiring and held back at the same time. His voice seemed higher, and he didn't tower over me the way I'd felt he had when we were young. But it was his all-in happiness to be in my company that I could not reconcile with the aloof kid who broke my teenaged heart.

D was in charge of the walk. I was happy to let go of navigation. He led me into the building that used to be called Rochdale; he'd lived in the student-run co-op-cum-free college, which became one of North America's biggest drug havens, from 1972 to 1975. It was rough going toward the end. Residents were under siege by the police for the final year, until everyone was forcibly evicted. But it had given D the confidence of a survivor. "Proved my cool courage or whatever." He took me up to the floor where he'd lived. As soon as we got off the elevator, I had a fully formed memory of having been there. And of having dreamed about this hallway many times since.

"I was here with you in 1972." We were standing outside his dorm room door.

"What? No."

"Your hands were covered in ink." The place was bringing back the memory, like the map of St. Catharines. The ink made my memory real to him too. He'd dropped out of medical school and was working at Rochdale's printing press, editing a newspaper and running off free university degrees for anyone who wanted one. "It was a very inky period," he said.

"I remember I was desperate to be cool when I came here, which I was not." I'd felt tremendous pressure, I didn't tell him, to know how to do things in bed, where we ended up—things I didn't know but people who lived in Rochdale likely did. I remembered his arms outstretched like Christ's on the cross as I attempted to be on top, or give him a blowjob, both unexplored terrain for me at eighteen.

"We must have bumped into each other on the street, and maybe you invited me?" Once again, we discovered our historical proximity to each other; while he was at Rochdale, I was living around the corner in an apartment with my sister Laura. "Right after that, I left for university," I told him.

"I wonder what would have happened if you hadn't?" He was running his hands over me, finding my outline under my coat. I zipped it open, not for him to touch me, but to see me so he'd stop touching me.

We left Rochdale and roamed the University of Toronto campus, drifting in and out of his time there as a medical student. When we stopped for tea, he reached into the chest pocket of his coat and brought out a small piece of paper, which he opened fold by fold to reveal a series of grouped words in an elegant, printed hand.

"Wait! You, a list?" In the top right corner, he had written the words "Wagner" and "bandwidth." "What's this part about?"

"It's the Cathrin corner."

"I have a corner?" Not only a list, but a spatially organized list, like a map. I was delighted. And I was at the top right, a significant place on a list. "What's it about?"

"Wagner because of rising tension without resolution, but the tension does eventually resolve when it hits the right note. You know, 'Liebestod' from *Tristan and Isolde*. 'Sex and death.'"

I knew only vaguely, but it felt true. D and I were different in many ways, most especially in how he saw the dark side and me the bright of our lives in Grimsby and ever since. But we were aligned around the intensity, maybe ferocity, with which we had pursued our careers in journalism and psychiatry, and pursued love too. "Maybe I moved toward light and you toward dark, and maybe together we made some kind of eclipse. If that's how eclipses work."

"Not really." A navigator and a keeper of the facts. I liked those things. And then this: "I never had a thing for Arlene. At all." And that's what it took, an ancient victory, to make my rictus smile disappear. I smiled happily at D. He kissed me.

When we finally ended our walk, D handed me a card with his phone number and address. "I'm trusting you aren't a stalker," he said as he put his card into my hands, and I could see that he shared some of my own fears. "Please call me."

I tucked the card into the kitchen drawer where I kept cards of repair people, doctors, and accountants. Maria, her wisdom imparted, had gone back upstairs to work, and I'd screwed the cap back on the wine with just enough left that I could tell myself I hadn't downed an entire bottle of Gavi in the middle of the afternoon. Then I opened a post-walk email from D:

Parallel lives. I think I got a bit overwhelmed by you. I hope I was not too physical.

I took off my bulky black coat, finally, and sat down at the kitchen table to write my final email to D. Clarity was kindness, I'd decided, and it was better to tell him immediately how

I felt. I wrote that the intensity in our emails was also there in person, and that it was too much for me. My own bandwidth—his word on the list to stress his need for privacy—was becoming narrower all the time. I'd been wrong to think I could take love on again at sixty-eight. I told him I was sorry we went as far as we did in our emails, giving over so much without really knowing each other. *I loved your list. It was perfect. Wagner.*

He wrote back with his own clarity that he was sorry to lose our mutual regard, and that he admired me for making a decision and following through with it—*so no blame. Please know that this was real. We created love by writing to each other.* And then he went decisively quiet.

In that silence over the next couple of weeks, I began to consider the man I had met that afternoon. My scared-rabbit panic had made me decide on sight that I'd fallen for someone I didn't know and for a future I didn't want. A future that held nothing but fragility for a pair of seventy-year-olds.

But what did fragility matter? Or rather, wasn't it all that mattered?

I went to my bookshelf and took down Elizabeth Strout's *Olive Kitteridge.* Olive was one of my favorite characters. She took up so much space you couldn't stop thinking about her, even when she wasn't in the scene. When I first met her on the page, she was older than me; we're closer in age now. (In that book at least; Olive continues to age in each of Strout's books that come after.)

I sat at my kitchen table and flipped to the last chapter, called "River." In it, Olive, seventy-four and widowed, is unexpectedly drawn to her neighbor Jack Kennison, also widowed and a retired academic snob she'd long despised. Stomach bulging like a sack of sunflower seeds, balding head thrust forward when he walked—Old Horror was her name for him. She railed against him. She listed his flaws to her friend on the phone. She lay awake "at the age of seventy-four and thought about his arms around her." After an intermittent and often angry courtship, she sat beside him on his bed one afternoon and put her hand over his heart, a heart that someday soon would stop. "But that someday was not now."

"What young people didn't know, she thought, lying down beside this man, his hand on her shoulder, her arm; oh, what young people did not know." This was the passage I had been looking for. "They did not know that lumpy, aged, and wrinkled bodies were as needy as their own young, firm ones, that love was not to be tossed away carelessly, as if it were a tart on a platter with others that got passed around again. No, if love was available, one chose it, or didn't choose it."

I paced around the house for a long time after I read that passage. What an extraordinary occurrence, I thought, to have met this person from my long-ago past, to resurface the belowground feeling from when I was a girl. It began to seem more like a gift than a danger to meet someone with the cool courage to face whatever was coming next. It made me remember that part of myself, the unafraid part, the part I'd need with less time ahead than behind. Meeting D had made the present feel roomier than the future, just when I was grappling with how much future I had left.

I'd run away from the chance to take the old story to a new place. I'd thrown away the tart. The longer D was gone, the more I understood that I'd missed him when we met, and now was missing him.

ten

A TALLY, PART 2: OLD BODY POLITICS

"AUNT CATHRIN, I FEEL UNCOMFORTABLE when you body-shame."

My niece Keogh was washing local lettuces for dinner at our rented ranch house on Hornby Island, a three-ferry trip into the Pacific Ocean off the coast of British Columbia. Outside the kitchen window the sea slowly came in for the second time that day, cooling the flat rocks that had basked in the sun all afternoon, and us along with them. We'd sat side by side on our lawn chairs when I drew Ann's attention to someone walking a dog on the distant rocks by poking her in the arm.

"Ow!" she protested loudly. I poked her again. "*Ow!*"

"Now you know how it feels," I said.

"Maybe what you two should do"—Keogh, lying on a rock in her bikini, didn't look up as she said this sleepily to her mother and aunt—"is have a physical fight."

Ann turned in her chair to take me in. She had a way of putting her body into her words. "I would so win."

"You left out the part where you flung your folding chair on the ground and stomped around." This was Laura, later.

"What?" But it was already coming back to me. I'd been having some difficulty relaxing into the mellow vibe of the remote hippie island. I'd woken up hard from a nap to discover my sisters had gone ahead to the water with the easier-to-manage folding chairs. (Opening complicated beach chairs is a competitive sport on the Canadian West Coast.) No one helped me with mine, so I threw my complex mini-lounger across the rocks and demanded my younger sister open it. And after she did, I poked her.

Ann and I did not fist-fight that day. I dislike losing any kind of contest and the prospect of being hit, both of which seemed inevitable in a tussle with my younger sister, who invited me to feel her abs, which were as hard as the rock under our chairs. And also Ann, with her indefatigable energy and good cheer and still-undaunted forward momentum, had been the one to organize this trip, loading her small orange Suzuki with two sisters, two teenagers, two bikes, and then driving us to this beautiful house that she had found for our holiday. But I admired the sageness of Keogh's fistfight idea. One of the grabby things about being older is witnessing my daughter and nieces develop personalities and wisdom to contend with. I was not about to dismiss anything that came from my daughter's mouth, or Keogh's either.

But body-shame? I couldn't think what I might have said to make my niece feel that way. I'd spent a lot of time not just thinking about women's bodies and the freedom with which we commented on them but shutting down any such comment that came from my own mouth. I'd never have said anything negative about Keogh's body, I was sure of that. The beautiful young splendor of her, for one thing. But I wouldn't have said that out loud either.

When I was thirty years younger, a low whistle, a wink, and buckled knees were hallway hellos at the newspapers where I worked. I had no complaints about being casually sexualized; it was fun and lusty and a little dangerous. Being admired for your body, and dressing to be admired for your body, was validating, I thought, before the male gaze became taboo.

Worse things went on, things that were demeaning to have been complicit in, because women carried the false shame that we had brought it on ourselves. One woman was asked to spin around in a job interview so the boss could see her from all sides, another to try on a tight T-shirt to help him decide whether to feature it in a magazine, another to lift her red boot onto the boardroom table in a news meeting for everyone's comment. "Don't tug that skirt down on my account," a boss said to me when I noticed it had ridden up. I blushed and didn't.

"A colleague asked me if I could move my hair so he could admire my necklace." Jumping ahead thirty years, the person speaking held out a delicate gold necklace from her chest.

"Good of him to ask," I'd said, and meant it. "What'd you say?"

"I told him to fuck off."

"Straight to 'Fuck off'?"

"It was gross. And completely inappropriate."

She also told me, not unkindly, that women her age didn't appreciate the way women my age continually commented on their youth and looks, bodies and beauty. That we were sexualizing and objectifying them the same way men had us (and still did them). My first thought was: You're going to miss the hubba-hubba days when you're seventy. My second was that I'd become the old witch in *Hansel and Gretel*. "Give me your finger so I can tell if you're fat enough to cook!" I immediately self-corrected. Now I mostly wouldn't compliment another woman's looks. Instead, the compliment might be about the pleasure of her company and, maybe, "That's a cool bag." It's not just that I'd modified my behavior. I'd seen the good sense in modifying it. So this body-shaming thing brought me up short.

"I certainly didn't intend to do that to you, Keogh."

"Not my body, Aunt Cathrin. Yours."

My hand, on its way to my mouth with a cracker full of brie, paused in midair. We sisters and Keogh were scarfing dips and cheese and wine while hungrily preparing a dinner of fresh fish and salads for ourselves and Ann's other daughter, Claire, who was about to arrive with her two best friends from the tiny inland cabin they were sharing.

"Oh. Huh. My body. Right." I swallowed my cracker and did a quick mental survey of the things that had come out of my mouth in the past forty-eight hours: "When did my elbows start to sag?" "It's like my brown spots are propagating in the sun." "Do these flip-flops make my ankles look thick?" As the comments were about me, I felt I had a right to them. But if I was constantly assessing myself, it would follow that I was doing the same with everyone else. Putting down my body slammed my niece back into hers. As if she didn't have enough pressure to spend every moment assessing that body—skin, belly, thighs—in the social-media advertising capitalist stream in which we swam, undefended, like the fish in the ocean outside this kitchen window. The body scrutiny is merciless for the young and perfect, let alone the old and soft.

I loaded up another cracker—everything was so much more delicious after hours on the salty Pacific—and pulled myself back from saying I'd gained five pounds on this trip. Maybe it wasn't Keogh's body image I needed to think about. Maybe I was missing something important in the old-body putdowns. "Be on the alert to recognize your prime at whatever time of your life it may occur," wrote

Muriel Spark in *The Prime of Miss Jean Brodie* in 1961. Maybe, for me, that time was right now, and my body, for all its decrepitude, was part of that prime.

"Okay," I said to my niece. "I get what you're saying." I filled my glass, ready to hunker down into this particular conversation, but Keogh had already moved on, with the galloping speed of twenty-two.

"I wonder if you all would like to try mushrooms tonight?" She looked up from her lettuces and smiled winningly at her mother and aunts.

"I love sautéed mushrooms," said Laura.

"No, magic mushrooms," said Keogh.

"Mashed mushrooms?" I said.

"*Magic* mushrooms," Keogh repeated.

"Oh. No, thank you," Laura and I said in unison.

"I felt it was an on-topic idea," Keogh said later, "because mushrooms can make you feel very comfortable in your body, and it might have been liberating." I was not shy around drugs in my youth, and I'd done mushrooms a few times. The first, when I was younger than Keogh, I lay on my back under a reaching elm tree and experienced a throbbing oneness with the universe. The last, married with kids, I lay on my back again, this time in my bathroom, deeply pondering whether I should order turquoise or teal tiles for the walls around the tub. Drugs tend to elevate wherever you are in your life. Now I was turning seventeen all over again with my new Old

Friend. Maybe we'd try mushrooms together. Maybe we'd end up in bed. Maybe it was time to do a tally of my old body.

When Mary was thirteen, I'd often find her staring at herself in the bathroom mirror. Not with mirror-face, testing out pretty, but open and intent, like she was receiving something. She was the reflection of Mary and the receptacle of Mary, both at once. This could go on for an hour, maybe more.

"What are you doing?" I would have been sucked into the unquenchable fire of hell if I'd tried something similar at her age (after being bludgeoned to death by the six other family members trying to use the bathroom). But Mary wasn't vain, merely gathering evidence.

"I'm trying to figure out who I am."

"A child's body is very easy to live in." Ursula K. Le Guin started a blog when she was eighty-one; this is from one of her posts. "An adult body isn't. The change is hard. And it's such a tremendous change that it's no wonder a lot of adolescents don't know who they are. They look in the mirror—that is me? Who's me?

"And then it happens again, when you're sixty or seventy."

After the Hornby trip, called up short on my body-shaming and feeling I would perhaps soon need to look my best unclothed, I decided to do my own mirror study. To take another tally, this one of my body as it was at sixty-eight.

That is me. Who is me? I would become rememberable to myself as I was now, without censure, transitioning to old age as Mary had to teen age.

I undressed quickly and stared at myself in my full-length bedroom mirror, pen and paper in hand to do my tally, until I realized I'd gotten to know mirror me a little too well. She aimed to please. She attracted me to me. Even now, old and stripped, she smiled wryly at me. *Could be worse,* she said. *Nice shoulders.*

I wanted something more antagonistic, or at least less pliable, than the way the mirror let me shift and dodge and adjust to how I looked. I thought about Lucian Freud's naked painting of himself at seventy-one. "I seldom got so fed up with a model," he said, and he does look impatient and combative, his head thrust forward for battle, as he stands and faces us, literally cocky. *The New Yorker*'s Adam Gopnik wrote that with his naked paintings, Freud wanted "fully realized art of dense contemplation and diligent inspection that did not wince or pause at a single human fold, wrinkle, or pelvic peculiarity."

I quickly took several pictures in my full-length bedroom mirror of the front and the back of me. I was no Lucian Freud, but these photos would do for my purposes. I got dressed, sat on the bed with my pen and paper close at hand, and flipped through my phone. I winced so hard my face cramped, and without pause, I deleted them. "Christ," I said out loud.

I texted Ann to call me.

I'm in a weird small airport lounge no privacy, she texted back. She was on her way to New Orleans. *Want to talk via text?*

Ann did study her body, she texted me, and obsessed over changes for the worse. *That soft skin near my armpit. The slight sagging beginning at the tip of my inner thighs.* As she got older, she shared the regret of every woman in the Milky Way that she'd never embraced the beauty of her younger body. *Mom was pivotal in passing on our body insecurity. She had it horribly as did her mom and the whole f'in chain of oppression that keeps women in this cycle of body-shaming because of unattainable standards of beauty. I've had to learn to not do that to my girls because it runs deep.*

We're gonna board. Send questions.

I asked her if she still looked at her vagina regularly, a bit off-topic but a minor obsession of mine after my doctor told me women under sixty were checking out their vaginas in mirrors at least once a week. (My own research bore this out. Every woman under sixty answered, unvaryingly, "Of course." Women sixty and up tended not to appreciate the question. Which was odd, because a lot of those women were part of the original consciousness-raising, hold-a-mirror-to-the-vagina 1960s.)

I do, not just my VJ but the whole area. PS: I'm not going to take naked photos. The front cameras on phones are hideous if you're taking a selfie. A regular camera should be more forgiving.

Ann was right. I needed better-quality naked photographs, and the solution was near at hand. Mary's degree was in photography. She often made photo studies of herself, and sometimes of me, for a newspaper or magazine. Clothed, of course. She was an excellent photographer, with an unerring eye for the right light to show her subjects at their best.

"Hey, Mary, I wonder if you could do something for me?"

We were at the Toronto Eaton Center on a Saturday night, looking for a dress for a wedding Mary was attending. It had to be pink and it had to be full length, the bride said. Mary and I were both fed up from too many failures in airless fitting rooms and had paused for Diet Coke and end-of-day 30 percent off sushi in the basement food court of the downtown mall. This was our second expedition on the same quest.

"I'm so tired of this hunt." Mary was despondent.

"We'll find the dress," I said. We had two months before the wedding. "Don't despair."

"I'm definitely despairing. But I appreciate your confidence."

Mary had been telling me between dressing rooms that she couldn't put me and her father in nursing homes "when the time came." After she won the lottery, she was going to buy a massive estate with separate wings for everyone. "You'll be in one wing and Dad in the other, so you'll never have to see or speak to each other." Which was not unlike the last ten years of our marriage, I didn't say, minus the separate wings. Mary was the family glue. This was not a small undertaking in the long aftermath of divorce. She talked to everyone and did her best to keep the rest of us talking too. Her sweet concern for my future made me brave about asking my question. She'd been thinking about how things were trending for me, age-wise.

"I wonder," I said on the bench at the bottom of the down escalator in the basement of the mall, "if you could take some photographs of me naked?"

Mary's head snapped up.

"NO!! *MOM!!!*" She took one gasping breath. "Do I have to? I mean, what's it for? Is it for a doctor? I mean, if it's for a doctor and there's some horrible growth or something you need a picture of, I could do that. But just your naked body? *Mom!*"

I explained that I was trying to do a tally of my old body, and was upset to see how much worse I looked in my photos than in the mirror.

"That's the same for everybody," Mary said. When you look in the mirror you don't see yourself as you are seen. It has nothing to do with age." She looked worried. Likely she was reconsidering the nursing home. "God. Mom!!"

"So that's a no?"

"*Hard* no." Mary calmed herself and pointed her chopsticks down to the bench. "Are you going to eat that last piece of sushi?"

—

I called Laura, who'd joined those consciousness-raising, vagina-inspecting groups in the 1960s. I'd never forgotten what she told me. It was around the time that D was living a block away in Rochdale (and I was having terrible sex with him). Laura said that one of the women told the group that she had orgasms if a man merely touched her breasts. Setting off thirty years of my own panic. "I think those vagina sessions came out of the book *Our Bodies, Ourselves*, from the Boston Women's Health Collective," Laura told me on our call.

"Do you look at yourself naked in the mirror anymore?" I asked her.

"Absolutely not. I'm considering taking down the mirror in my hallway so I don't have to see myself under any circumstances. Seventy-five is not the new forty-five. My body didn't get the memo on that one."

Laura remembered a visit to our aunt Helen when she was ninety. We were at either end of our fifties and already feeling ancient. Helen was the middle sister between Aunt Mary and Mom, and the one I was told I most resembled. "She liked to have an anecdote ready for us," Laura said. "A little stand-up routine she'd perfect before we arrived."

On this early spring visit, Helen told us she'd just done a checkup on her body after the long winter, to see how things were trending. "I took off every stitch and stood stark naked in front of the full-length mirror." *Every stitch, stark naked*— old turns of phrase that suggested nakedness was a rare occurrence for my aunt. Not to be confused with a lack of interest in her appearance, which Helen took great care of until she died at ninety-seven. She skillfully thrift-shopped and kept up with trends. On this visit she had on a pair of laced brogues, ribbed tights, a kiltish wool skirt to the knee, and a fitted heather sweater. Her hair done, as always. When I worried my daughter was vain, I was only fifty. I thought vanity—self-love, self-regard, self-admiration—was something to keep secret. Especially when you had a reason for it, being as beautiful as Mary. And then let go of when you no longer had a reason for it. I didn't understand the enduring importance of vanity, no matter how old you got. Do we stop dressing pleasingly at seventy because we've been liberated from the male gaze? Of course not.

(I'm less sure about men. Laura and I went to see a famous local poet give a talk at eighty. "Maybe he can no longer see well enough to brush his hair?" I said, because it was standing straight on end, with the stage lights giving him a mad-king corona. "He hasn't brushed his hair since he was eighteen," Laura said.)

"What's this doing way down here, and why is that over there!" Laura and I loved the memory of Helen's body tally. The legs were the last to go, she had said. And: "No man wants to look at an old woman's flat ass in a pair of pants." She'd been shopping with a young friend who still looked terrific in jeans, she told us, and bought two pairs at

Helen's urging. "How old is she?" I'd asked. "Seventy-six," Helen told us.

"I immediately bought a new pair of jeans when we got home," I told Laura on the phone. (After my sister and I hung up, I was pushed a *New Yorker* cartoon of two women talking in front of a grave: "His last words were, 'Yes, Dear, those jeans make you look fat.'")

"You two are so young." I remembered the grip of my aunt's knobby hand on my arm as she held tight to Laura and me, ancient in our fifties, when we said goodbye at her side door. Not witchy hands but strong hands from a lifetime of work. "You glorious girls. Enjoy youth while you have it."

The front door of the Hornby Island beach house swung open, and Claire and her two friends, Zoë and Jane, arrived for dinner. They were best friends in high school and now lived together in Montreal while attending Concordia University. Ann and I had visited them there, and I couldn't get enough of them. Jane was studying to be a filmmaker, Zoë a painter, and Claire a writer, they told us, and I loved how unafraid they were to see themselves as they wanted to become, to imagine their best and most hopeful dreams of their future. I was certain they would not falter.

They swooped through our roomy wooden beach house like swallows, exclaiming over the floor and the local island art on the walls. Jane, alert and dark-haired, stood over the old upright piano and began a delicate composition she was working on. Zoë, tall and freckled, joined her, and they switched to a Philip Glass piece. They were nineteen and twenty, worried about turning twenty-one, and I tried to remember what that particular concern felt like. It was a passage, I dimly recalled. Not unlike my own at the other end.

I was so absorbed by their energy and joy, by the way everything in the simple beach house took on a shine as they glanced off it, I said, "I don't know, you're all just so glorious." Maybe getting in the way of their unconsciously free and easy selves. Free to be as they are now, and to become whoever they might be in their long lives ahead. Maybe it was time to channel my twenty-year-old self, or the seventeen-year-old me that D had uprooted. Maybe she would help me give birth to my old age. I know she had her own fears and worries, like my niece and her friends. But also like them, she was brave and strode into her life, for whatever came next.

What is age but becoming who you are? Like Mary looking for herself in the mirror at thirteen. Like Helen doing the same at ninety, and me at sixty-eight. I never did write down my tally of the old me, but I carry her. The crone "must become pregnant with herself, at last." That's Le Guin's blog again. "She must bear herself, her third self, her old age, with travail and alone.

"Not many will help her with that birth."

—

Seven women went down to the sea before dinner as the in-coming tide began to create tiny pools of life in the hollows of the rock. Laura and Ann and I mostly stood still and watched the girls—we tried not to call them girls to their faces—as they explored the tide pools like little kids, ebullient, their high voices singing over the rocks. Zoë, the youngest at nineteen, crunched on the barnacles in bare feet "to toughen them up." (I bought my third por-trait of a woman from her on this trip, Zoë's first sale as a painter. "I will remember this my whole life," she said when I handed her the check.) Claire fell in love with a tiny rock-colored crab. Jane took pictures. The glasses of white wine we each held were goblets of fire in the setting sun, we the flamebearers.

"Tell us your story as sisters," Jane said to Laura, Ann, and me after dinner as we sat and talked at an upstairs window with a cinematic view of the wilding sea. But we got onto first kisses instead, however that happened. Laura kissed her first boyfriend, Mickey (who turned out to be D's older step-brother from his mother's late-life love match, another path crossing), on the footbridge over the tumultuous spring creek in Grimsby. Ann won the longest kisser contest in eighth grade. She couldn't remember the boy, but the song was "Stairway to Heaven." My first kiss, at Expo 67, was with a handsome French-Canadian boy, dancing to "A Whiter Shade of Pale." Claire looked up both songs on her phone:

"Seven minutes and four minutes long." We never got to our story as sisters except to say we were three of five siblings. "All from the same parents?" asked Jane. Which I thought was a very modern question.

The young women told us that older men, in their thirties, had started to harass them on the beach. This had never happened to them on Hornby before, and they were interested in why it was happening now. They'd decided it was because it was the first time they'd been to the island without parents. They didn't worry that it was their own slenderly clad bodies that had brought on the unwanted attention. They'd laid down that particular burden, long carried by their mothers and aunts, that they were responsible for men's behavior toward them.

By now, the waves were crashing loudly and the rocks were completely submerged. We watched out the window as two little boys from next door came screaming down the path and jumped into the foam, crazy with happiness. Jane stood up suddenly, as if shaken awake by the shouts.

"We have to go."

"Ten more minutes," said Ann. We couldn't bear for them to leave, like Helen with Laura and me.

"No. Now." Jane was unconquerable. "Or we'll miss the sunset on Grassy Point."

All three girls raced out the door, as excited as the boys in the surf. Maybe to catch themselves on Jane's camera in the best ocean light, we didn't know. A year later, I'd be back on the Pacific Ocean, with the same women and at the same tenuous time of night, for Jane's memorial. She died from a sudden and unstoppable sickness a few months after she turned twenty-one. We sat on a blanket by the shore to make small candlelit boats bearing messages for Jane and then launched them into the water with dozens more. The lanterns of Jane's parents and younger sister were the first out, leading all the other lanterns into the bay, until just one was going ahead of the rest, with travail and alone.

eleven

THE LONG TAIL OF DIVORCE

What is taken apart is not utterly demolished.

It is like a great mysterious egg in Kansas

that has cracked and hatched into two big bewildered birds.

TONY HOAGLAND, "In Praise of Their Divorce"

———————————

"I'M BRINGING OVER PHOTOGRAPHS I found in the basement." Some kind of spell had come over Laura, a restless impulse to root around in the backs of drawers and top-shelf boxes. "You're the right person for Dad's wool blanket." "I'm dropping off Aunt Mary's dinner plates." "The baby's going to love this plastic pumpkin. It lights up, see?" She rarely arrived empty-handed. "Laura, do not leave that plastic pumpkin here," I said. (She did. The baby loves it.)

Laura was in a big cull, absorbed in the process of going through a life's accumulation of things. I was not in a big cull, not in my house and certainly not in the life I'd made for myself since my divorce. My pin was on the map. I'd decided staying put really was an active decision, not digging in but digging down. Until this basement-box discovery of Laura's.

The leaves were mostly done falling, with only the laggards hanging on. It was a cool and still October afternoon as my sister and I sat side by side in garden chairs. (It was a phase of the pandemic when we were all going back and forth on indoor vs. outdoor visits; this was an outdoor time.) To our right were the hornbeam trees, tall and thin like gangly teenagers. I thought of them as my sentries, standing guard. They'd grow into the job.

"Some people believe hornbeams have heartbeats. They troop through the woods with stethoscopes trying to listen to them," I said. We talked about trees while the photographs waited in Laura's lap for their moment. My sister had a story to tell me, and I was happy to let her find the pace. I used to be impatient to fast-forward to the action in conversations. I often wished I had a clicker. Around sixty-five, you realize the pauses are where all the action is.

"I found these from when you were newly married." Laura opened the envelope with care and placed the first picture in my open hands. "Look how young you are." I looked like a woodland animal, small, with alert brown eyes, thick eyebrows, and glossy dark hair. I'd recently watched *The*

Beatles: Get Back documentary series, and all I could talk about afterward was their hair. It was lustrous, like freshly poured tar. I asked my niece Claire what products she used to get her hair as shiny as the Beatles', and she said, "It's just my hair, Aunt Cathrin." So that was the first thing I noticed in the first photograph: my shiny young hair.

My husband and I were in the center of the frame, holding each other's hands on Laura's couch. In the next picture, his arm is draped over my shoulder and he's laughing. "Look how happy!" Laura said. An American scientist named Dr. John Gottman followed thousands of couples for twenty years and concluded that the end of a marriage is contained in its beginning. Eye rolls, blinking, interruptions, fidgeting at the start of a relationship predict divorce; watching, listening, smiling, touching, a long and happy marriage. The way my husband's looking at me in these early pictures, he should be singing me to sleep tonight.

"Now watch. Look how he's begun moving to the edges." Laura put a series of pictures in my hands, one after another. Ten, then twelve, then fifteen years passed, and instead of being in the center of the frame, my husband gradually began to step away until, in every picture, he was on the periphery. The kids were young, our home was filled with family and friends, and we had the life we'd wanted. But the evidence was in my hands, impossible to unsee: his steady movement out of the frame.

After Laura left (with the pictures; culling is a personal process, and only you know what to keep and what to pass on), I thought about that watchful young woman in those early photographs. I recognized right away who she was and what she'd wanted: that man beside her, and the life they were going to make together. What caught me off guard was the slow-moving thought that I didn't know myself nearly so well forty years later. The pictures, freighted for having been in a box for so many years, showed the long tail of the dissolution of my marriage. But—and this was a deeply unwelcome idea—was the tail of my divorce even longer? To put it another way: My divorce had freed me from my husband, but did it free *me*? Was I still, in some way I hadn't understood, essentially married?

About a year after my husband and I separated, a newsroom colleague whose marriage had ended many years before my own gave me a formula for when I'd be over the end of my twenty-five-year marriage. Never mind the experts who said it would be eighteen months. Take the number of years you'd been married and divide by two. "It's a long road," she said matter-of-factly, and went back to typing.

By her math, depending on whether I count from my separation or my legal divorce, I'm somewhere between fully over it and four more years to go. I've at least found the strange serenity shared by most long-divorced people, who say things like "I don't know why, really," or "Divorce, it's such a mystery."

They don't want their marriages back. Don't be ridiculous. But they've had a reasonable enough interlude to allow them to think reasonably about divorce.

Nutshell, Ian McEwan's story of Hamlet as told by a fetus, is set in the year of my own divorce. I read it the minute it came out, partly because it was a genius idea and partly because I wanted to see what he had to say about marriage. "When love dies and marriage lies in ruins," the fetus propounds as his mother and uncle plot to poison his father, "the first casualty is honest memory, decent, impartial recall of the past. Too inconvenient, too damning of the present." Things between the narrator's parents get so bleak—it's *Hamlet,* after all—that at one point, the fetus tries to hang himself with his own umbilical cord. McEwan was divorced himself. The courts were involved. I trusted he'd been to the darkest places a marriage can take a person when he went on to say, "So, against that headwind of forgetfulness I want to place my little candle of truth and see how far it throws its light."

By understanding my marriage, I'll finally understand my divorce and be done with it. I'll go in there with my own little candle of truth, picking through the ruins. Whether I can trust myself is another question.

My marriage began well, and I'm thankful for that. Not all love stories do, and in this time when I was thinking so much about the end of love, books that took me to love's beginnings kept landing on my bedside table. "They'd been going out for a whole month, him fairly killing himself to get out on the bus or the train to her," wrote Sebastian Barry of Tom Kettle's courtship of his wife in *Old God's Time*. "Oh bejesus, but he had to gallop all the way across Dublin, through the Green, down Grafton Street, skirt the college, stampede up Abbey Street and on to Talbot, and go like the clappers to Connolly station for the 5.30 to Bray . . . After a month of this he might have qualified for the Irish team at the Olympics."

Right after I finished Barry's book, I read Claire Keegan's *So Late in the Day*, where her narrator recalled his courtship: "Little more than a year ago, he had almost run down the stairwell from the office to meet Sabine." *Almost* run. Has there ever been a more succinct description of withholding? It seemed to me, reading those books back-to-back, that all of love's beginnings were contained between them, the boundless and the boundaried.

Mine was the first kind. Likely these stories of happier days in my marriage are watercolor, but I'll give myself that at least. I'd take stairs two at a time and fly into him if he'd been away a few days. Biking, skiing, canoeing. Rapids! "Where are you going to drag her next?" his father said, not kindly, but it was true. He took me out. Along the river, onto the road, into the world of motion. I'd have followed him anywhere. I pedaled my bike in his wake after he taught me how to catch his slipstream. When my arms got too tired to paddle the canoe, I'd lie back on the duffel bags and watch the sun make polka dots on his face as he soundlessly sterned, cigarette dangling from his mouth. He was very handsome.

"I can stand on the gunnels and perfectly balance there without tipping," he said, it was a camp trick, on our first night on the Spanish River in Northern Ontario. I figured it was the wine-from-a-box talking; we were cooking dinner.

"Cannot," I said. Canoes are famously tippy, never more so than when you grab hold of the gunnels. ("Let go of the gunnels!" he'd yell when I'd freeze in the roaring rapids.) I turned the potatoes in the fire as he paddled into a lee in the river. He slowly pulled himself up to crouch on the gunnels, then rose, all legs like an egret, blond hair bleached white from the sun in a crest on top of his head. "Ta-da," he said softly. And then the canoe didn't tip but slowly sank under his weight, him still standing on the gunnels, grinning, until he was waist-deep in water. I fell off my log laughing. The potatoes got burnt.

HOLY MATRIMONY said the handwritten banner on the wall behind us at our wedding rehearsal. There's a picture of this too. We're holding hands, him leaning low against the church piano so he didn't loom over me. "I hate to think of that man's long legs wasted on you in bed," tall drunk women would say to me as they leaned on him at parties. I watched as he leaned them back up. In the pre-wedding picture, we were young-thin and shiny from the heat—we got married on a burning August day in a church on the Niagara River. I'd wanted to run off together. But my husband believed marriage was a public act and needed a community to witness it, and I understood that public-spiritedness as we said our vows and people sang and prayed in unison, or you might say in community, behind us. We were doing something bigger than ourselves. We both marveled afterward how we'd felt lifted to another place, somewhere more spacious and with import, like pausing at the top of a grand staircase just before you entered the ball. It felt like it really was *Holy Matrimony,* and something to live up to.

And we did, for a long time. Our plan was to have four children. When years passed without one, we struggled through infertility treatments and failed attempts at adoption. We were as one in this, never faltering in our hope to create a family. I've forgiven but not forgotten the man who said to me, "Adoption? So you did it the easy way." Eight years later, when we finally adopted our son and then our daughter, I would wake up frightened by how lucky we were, our happy, hard won family. His parents had a northern cottage, and we all four slept in the loft, beds in a row. At home, all our bedroom doors were left open for the goodnight ritual:

Good night, Mummy. I love you.
Good night, Daddy. I love you.
Night night, sleep tight. Don't let the bedbugs bite.

Until the time came when all the doors were shut at night, in the false hope that the kids wouldn't hear the terrible words that were being said behind them.

It's a big jump from the beginning of love to the end. It's just that the middle is as much a slog to describe as it is to live through. *Anatomy of a Fall,* French director Justine Triet's marriage drama, puts the wife on trial for the murder of her husband, but really, it's marriage that's on trial. Marriage was the murderer. Only one could survive it.

We see the couple's sexy, laughing beginnings in photographs like the ones Laura showed me of me and my husband. And then we skip over the rest of the marriage to maybe fifteen years later, the day before his death, while the husband's aggressive steel drum track clangs and crashes in the background. We watch the couple in their kitchen and understand the long unwinding of their relationship in one brilliantly written and brutal argument, which ends off camera when the fight becomes physical. We hear but don't see her smash a wineglass and slap him in the face; we hear him grunt as he grabs and bruises her wrist and hits himself in the head over and over before punching a hole in the wall. It's as good a portrayal I've seen or read of the bleak middle of a marriage, simply by leaving things out. We can fill in the blanks. Our own marriages do that for us.

An insult at a dinner party, a punishing silence after the guests leave, a slow dwindling of the pillow talk that might have put things to rights. A first "Fuck you," a new stinginess around compliments, a nose-to-nose spitting argument, a dalliance, a lie, a chasmic betrayal. Birthdays were the worst. Christmas was the worst. Mornings were the worst. Dinner was the worst. Bed—oh god, bed!—was like being on two sides of enemy lines while sharing the same mattress. The person you once loved more than any other is now in a war with you, and you don't know how you got here, or how to get out. I don't remember when he began to refer to me as "she" and "her," as if saying my name was too personal for what existed between us. I do remember my dread the day I arrived home after my third session with the psychiatrist who was urging me to leave my marriage. "It's bricks and mortar," he'd said when I told him I was too afraid to lose my children, house, friends. Life. "Bricks and mortar," he kept saying, and I had a kind of sleep-death there in his office—my eyes became heavy, my head bobbed—and it's a blank how I got from there to my front hallway, where I tripped on my husband's size 13 shoes flopped inside the door. Oh no, I thought into the thick silence of the house. He's home.

Most wives loathe their husbands for a good ten-year stretch somewhere around the middle of a long marriage. We fantasize about their funerals after their not-too-painful deaths (so the children don't suffer). Years earlier, I'd wept in the passenger seat as my husband was driving, sorrowfully planning the flowers for his imaginary send-off. And then he told me about my funeral, which he attended alone and forlorn. "Seriously?" I said, blowing my nose. "Nobody came but you?" But those were happier times. Friendships formed like book clubs around all the ways wives hated their husbands. "I play the piano for hours and hours, weeping over how much I hate him," said one woman in those years, maybe in our late forties. And then she came out the other side to a pretty good marriage. Twenty years later, the piano-weeping was a bad patch.

"Out of the frying pan, into the fire, into the inferno of the center of the earth, into the sun, into a distant star," said a happily married young man over a sparkling cold glass of Sancerre in my kitchen, startling the hell out of me. Had he read my mind? I'd been thinking a lot about my marriage before he came over, and my attention had drifted as he'd described a holiday he'd taken. I was back in that lethal middle of my marriage, and this young friend had just nailed what it was like in there: not even the sun is big enough to contain the sadness and fury. Maybe the distant stars can finally burn it out.

"Right?" I said.

"Totally. That's what it was like looking into the Grand Canyon."

There's a great distance between a bad patch and a grand canyon.

—

"I know we had happy days in our marriages, but it's hard to remember them," Ellen told me as we walked through the city with Sally tall and erect between us, avoiding the streets where we'd once lived happily with our husbands because they made us sad. She'd been separated for twenty-eight years, me fifteen, and our marriages were as steady a subject as our mothers, more as time passed. "It's unbearable to think about how it must have hurt our children."

I told Ellen then about being on the Spadina streetcar with Mary a couple of days earlier when an angry passenger got on. "He was walking down the aisle; we were walking up. I clocked his anger but didn't think much about it as I brushed past him."

"You can be oblivious," said Ellen.

"Yes. So when Mary caught up with me—she'd sat down in a seat to let the man pass—she said, 'Mom! You need better self-awareness. That man was seriously out of it, and you kept walking as if nothing was going on.'"

"Our kids are so much smarter than we are."

"True. But I didn't really get how upset Mary was. She kept going on about how you must step aside to give an angry person all the room they need. I was happy for her hyperawareness, though. It seemed like an excellent survival instinct. I said to her, 'You know, your brother has this same skill; he sees danger before it happens. You didn't get it from me, but I admire it in both of you.'

"Mary looked out the window for a long time after that,"
I said to Ellen, looking straight ahead as I did. "Then she
said, 'Well, Mom, you didn't grow up the way we did.'"
Ellen stayed quiet as we walked side by side.

"But we did have happy times," I said. I wasn't sure if I
was defending my own marriage or Ellen's. "We have happy
pictures."

"I was looking at all my photographs this morning, my
whole life," Ellen said. "Some people had been cut out of
them." I'd heard about a person or two who had been unkind
to Ellen, a category you wanted to stay out of with my friend.
"I wondered who could've done that, and then I realized it
was me. I did it."

When my husband moved out, he tore himself from a
wedding photograph and left his ring on top of the half that
was me. I'm smiling happily, my arm looped through his now
disembodied one. At the time, I was surprised he cared
enough to make the gesture; I understand better now that
our divorce wounded him as much as it did me, maybe more.
But I got the point. It was as succinct a message as it was
visceral: I was one now, not two.

When we arrived at the corner of our street, where Ellen
turned north, me south, I told her I'd just read Iris Murdoch's
definition of love. It was in a review of Paul Murray's *The Bee
Sting*, yet another novel about family love (gone way wrong
in that book) that had landed on my bedside table; these

love stories were flocking to me like homing pigeons, the way writing about something draws everything pertinent to you. "Murdoch said love is the extremely difficult realization that other people are real."

"Ooh, I love that."

"Right?"

My husband and I had a good divorce. Or at least an ordinary one. No violence or restraining orders or financial brutality. The bardo most people go through when they change from coupled to single—the necessary portal of confusion, sadness, and burn-the-street-down rage before you get to the other side—I'd gone through that while I was still married. We behaved reasonably, divided our assets fairly. I remortgaged the house to buy him out. He bought a bungalow farther north near the water, with boats and bikes and skis and books, the life he said he'd always wanted. We took turns choosing what to keep from our thirty years together, with generosity and even warmth. But marriage is not over with the furniture-dividing. Neither is divorce.

Our mistake was not to leave each other sooner. We're culturally inculcated to believe that to end marriage is to fail at marriage. "The alp-weight of pain, emotional violence, and above all *failure*," said Martin Amis of his divorce in his brilliantly generous final book, *Inside Story*. I took much to heart from that often tender book, but I didn't agree with Amis about the failure. You need to get divorced to know how much better it is than a marriage where the parties are too frightened to move on. Too afraid of the divorce, not afraid enough of the marriage.

I wish my husband and I had been able to admire what we'd accomplished, been proud of the family we'd created, and then been brave enough to let each other go instead of staying together for another eight years, "to persist, to persist, to try again, in the face of so much disappointment." (Amis.) We imagined, wrongly, that ending our marriage would bring more pain to our family than it was already suffering. That our bad marriage, and not our decent selves, was what protected us. As I approach old age, I allow myself to linger on that regret, and the harm it caused my children.

At my first party as a single woman, the host paired me with another newly divorced woman. She was terribly sad. I was not sad, but felt I ought to be, when a plain-speaking friend with an open freckled face and clear gray eyes interrupted the conversation to shake my hand.

"Congratulations! You're very brave. You must be proud of yourself."

"I am. I am proud. Thank you." We stood like that in the center of the crowded room, smiling and pumping each other's hands. I felt like we were shooting out light in every direction, if anyone had glanced over to see it like the bystanders at the end of Tony Hoagland's poem, *"pointing at the sky and / saying,* Look."

My husband is real. I am real. We are divorced.

"I live a wild, savage life." This was that newsroom colleague who'd told me how long it would take to be over my marriage. We were on the phone as I looked out my kitchen window onto the row of hornbeam trees. A couple of seasons had passed, and they'd grown a bit.

"You mean, like, eating pizza out of the box?" My imagination was having trouble grasping the concept. I'd called her to ask how she'd adapted to life as a single older woman, but "wild" and "savage" were not the words that came to mind when I pictured her. She'd retired a couple of years before I did, from a career in journalism that had been a lot like my own. She had kids, grandkids, a loving relationship with her aged mother, men now and then, a voracious reading habit, and a put-together look, although it's true she had the kind of free and joyous laugh that made you feel anything is possible.

"I go anywhere," she said. And I remembered that the last time she came for dinner, she told me she'd taken to traveling the world, often at the last minute (cheaper that way), always alone. "I do anything. My house, however I want it. All my single friends are the same." Her voice was ringingly clear. "They live crazy, free lives. More and more all the time."

I thought again about Deborah Levy in *The Cost of Living*,

the second installment of her living autobiography. After her own divorce, she seemed to grow three sizes, like the Grinch's bursting Christmas heart. She took to roaring around London on her new e-bike, books and groceries bouncing. "It was hard not to whoop," she wrote. Once, her store-bought chicken bounced out of her carrier and got run over by a car; in a supreme example of going with the flow, she served flattened chicken for dinner that night. She'd arrive at parties at the far end of the city, hair undone, slipping on her excellent shoes as she walked to the door, looking . . . wild and savage, I'm guessing. I'm certain that e-bike sales to divorced women over sixty spiked after that book came out. I considered getting one myself. But they move really fast.

Herein lies my pause, the interlude just before the story takes a turn. I left my marriage. Not only that, I kept the bricks and mortar and my mostly coupled friends too. I didn't have to choose; I've often wanted to call that psychiatrist and tell him he was wrong about that. The end of my marriage didn't derail me, because I stayed on track, not with my husband but with what we'd built together, and my life post-divorce was pretty much the same as my life pre-divorce.

I built a hut in the backyard of the house where I once lived with my husband. I planted a row of ancient woodland hornbeam trees, and I watched them take root, digging in. But also, reaching up, higher all the time. Like I said, they're teenagers. They have a ways to go.

twelve

LOST PANTS

I WAS WATCHING A COUPLE bundle a baby into a stroller in the subway station before taking him out into the cold December afternoon. People can look urgent on subway platforms, with trains coming and going, but not my couple. It was like they were inside a snow globe, like the world was the size of them.

I was across the tracks on the southbound platform, headed downtown to buy a new pair of navy pants. They were northbound, far enough away that I could study them at my leisure. The father's back had a worn-out look as he strapped in the baby. His coat was scruffy. They'd fallen on hard times, perhaps. The mother silently bent to tuck blankets around the baby. "Intent" was the word that came to mind. They were intent on their baby, and I watched them intently. They could've been my son, daughter-in-law, and grandson, except they were too tired and threadbare.

But then, *wait a minute*—what happened next was like realizing that the bewildered elderly woman reflected in a storefront window in fact was me. That family across the tracks *was* my son, daughter-in-law, and grandson.

I shot my hand up to call "Hey!" but right then my train arrived, like fate stepping in. Not the kind that hurtles you into each other but the kind that keeps you apart; the sliding doors, ships-that-pass kind of fate. When I think about the sadness that came later, it's tied up with the afternoon my son and I missed each other across the tracks of the subway station.

I boarded my train and hurried to the window to wave, but by then they were pushing the stroller onto the elevator to leave the station. I grabbed my phone and took pictures—a futile exercise, but as I flipped through the photos, I could just make out the blur of Ivonne's orange trapper hat in the elevator. Ivonne loved that hat. "I always wanted a hat with flaps over the ears," she said, even when she was growing up in Guatemala, where it was "sunny every day and the breezes were always warm." It made her proud to describe her perfect weather, and then sad about the warmth she'd left behind, and her eyes filled with tears. But at least she'd moved to a climate where a hat with flaps over the ears made sense. The orange surprised me—it's a bright hat. She immediately embraced how cold Canada was and rarely wore gloves or a scarf. But always the hat.

Looking at the pictures of the orange hat as my subway headed south reminded me of the first time I saw an orange tree. Our family took a car trip when I was thirteen, driving from Grimsby to Sarasota, Florida. Our trips until then—all of us crammed into a Ford or a Dodge—had been to Northern Ontario, so this one to Florida to see my dad's dad was an epic adventure. I remember a single orange on a tree as a smudge of brightness from my backseat window. Florida was crazy exotic like that. That fleeting orange was what Ivonne's hat looked like in my picture through the glass of the elevator door. It came to me that she was wearing the sunshine from home on her head.

"Look at this!" I said to Kelly when I got back to our house later that night, with my excellent new pants wrapped in tissue in my shopping bag—French navy, with the hard-to-find fitted calf and an unexpected cuff. "It's Ivonne's trapper hat! We were on the Dupont subway platform at the exact same time."

Kelly made the same gesture he'd made the night Ivonne had gone into labor six months earlier, pushing both palms down in a "Shh, calm down" motion at 2 a.m. "I'm going to a yoga class," he said in a whisper, and then rested his face on his hands like a baby sleeping. "Ivonne's in the kitchen. She's tired, Mom. She needs some time to herself," he said, closing the door gently behind him.

"Look closely!" I said to Ivonne when I found her sitting at the kitchen table staring into space. I held my phone near her face and imagined her saying, "How did you get that picture!" Marveling.

"This hat is your beacon of hope!" I said. She smiled a little, but I saw then that she really was tired out and wanted to be alone.

I went to bed myself. Obviously, I was the only one marveling about the orange hat and Florida oranges and Guatemalan sunshine. How everything is random and meaningless, and then a thing like a blurred picture of a hat from a train can make it all feel connected and purposeful. It's a feeling that comes over me lately when I'm in transit, that flow of subways and cars and bikes and people, how everything moves in sync like a grand plan. And then the feeling passes and the sadness slips in.

Kelly and Ivonne moved in right off the plane from the mountains of northern Guatemala, where love had found them. Ivonne had just discovered she was pregnant, to everyone's surprise and delight, and Kelly was about to begin a promising new job in Toronto. They married in the living room seven months later, in the Covid lockdown days, Ivonne eight months pregnant and radiant in a red dress, Laura and me crying as they said their vows. "I've been saving these for you," I'd said to Kelly a few weeks earlier, holding the wedding rings his father and I had exchanged. "They are handmade green and yellow gold. See how beautiful they are." "You're not serious right not, are you?" he said. The long tail of divorce continues with the children is what I am saying here. His parents' rings had not lost the symbolism of a broken family for him. They had for me, though, so I later had Pam the jeweler melt down the wedding ring my husband had left behind and turn it into a necklace. My own wedding ring was instantly displaced from its original purpose when Pam put it on my baby finger instead of my ring finger. "There," she said. "Not a wedding ring anymore." I wore it like that for some time, but it was too big, and I lost it when it fell off.

A month after the wedding, the baby was born on an April morning as perfect as his fingers and toes, his sweet-smelling head and tiny bundled body. "He's a super chill baby," said Kelly as we sat in awe over the bassinet on the kitchen table, an assessment the baby would dispense with in the next forty-eight hours as his lungs let loose on the world. The baby grew, Kelly's career expanded, Ivonne deferred requalifying as a dentist in Canada to work raising their son, and I traded one kind of job for another, settling in to write in the backyard hut. We lived a busy, sometimes connected, sometimes separate, domestic life. We whistled around the house. "We're just so happy," I said to anyone who asked.

It's pertinent that on the day of the subway disconnect, Christmas was mere weeks away. I put a lot of pressure on Christmas. This one was going to be the Christmas from my childhood, the one I'd not managed to give my children. But then we all came down with Covid, even the baby. If we'd known those fevers and coughs and streaming noses were coming, we might have thought twice about having the conversation we did, when we did. It was the first domestic argument in our multigenerational living setup. And the last, because they moved out a month later.

"We're looking for our own place," said Kelly as we made our coffee in the kitchen (we each had our own system). "Actually, I think we've already found it." That had been the plan, to get their own place after a couple of years, but this was sudden news. Their unhappiness had begun small; it was not a surprise to any of us that our standards of tidiness were different, and that I could be a bit of a domestic boss about messes and that they had a majestic talent for creating them. But it had grown from there.

"We thought you'd want to be more involved as a grandmother," Kelly said. "We feel like we're boarders with you instead of a family. Like when I grew up. Everyone in their own rooms."

"Hiding from your dad's fury," I said.

"Not just his," he said. "I mean, you built a hut, Mom."

As I write this from the calm perspective of the middle distance, I'm surprised that at the time, I felt this conversation had come out of the blue. I'd considered it a small miracle, or as if I'd gotten something wholly undeserved, to have it all: A four-month-old grandchild and his parents living with me, plus a retreat for me alone in the backyard. My son wanting more grandmother (and mother) from me might have been a mirror-moment of encountering who I was in his eyes, at least temporarily. The limits of my emotional availability. But not only that. We were each going through enough upheaval to sink the most buoyant domestic ship. Me newly retired and frantically anxious about money; Kelly in the early and sometimes nerve-wracking days of a demanding new job. Ivonne contending with a country far from home and a language not her own. Add in new marriage, new book, and new human being, and the only surprising thing was that any of us got out alive. But you don't know any of those things when you are in the dark middle. All you know is confusion, failure, and sorrow.

Luckily, right after the conversation in the kitchen, Covid descended, so staying in bed for three days with weeping red eyes was what was going on anyway. When I finally came downstairs, Kelly had dragged himself out to buy a Christmas tree. I also see with the passage of time that this was a gesture that we could return to our Christmas plans. But then, I took it as an affront because it had been something we were supposed to do together, to mark the beginning of our perfect Christmas.

"Someday, you're going to weep at what you said to me

about not being happy," I said, weeping as I sat beside the beautiful tree.

"I think that's probably true," Kelly said, his head bent low.

We agreed to put our grievances and hard words behind us—they didn't have much choice in the face of my unabated sorrow—and didn't speak of our rift again as we got ready for Christmas. We were polite. We avoided confrontation. It was my safe place, but perhaps not theirs. I thought about getting Kelly a new winter coat as a Christmas gift, to replace the one that had looked worn on the subway platform. Instead I got him a pair of boots, because it was what he said he wanted.

We had our family Christmas, and shortly after that, they did move out. And then, not right away, Kelly wrote to say that he was taking space to decide how much a part of his life he wanted me to be. And then came a silence that knocked me flat.

"So Mrs. Hall, she's made his favorite cookies. From when he was a little boy?"

I was at dinner with a small group of good friends, all women, telling them the entire plot of an episode of the BBC show *All Creatures Great and Small*. Tears were pouring out of me. But these were good friends, and no one tried to stop me, even when they looked at each other with alarm. They knew how hard a show can hit you when you're raw from something in your life.

It's 1939. Mrs. Hall's son hasn't spoken to her in years, ever since she turned him in to the police for stealing from her employer. But having joined the navy, and thinking he might die in the war, he's written: "Dear Muther. It's been quite some time." He tells her he'll meet her at a train station on his way to his ship. She sits at the station for many hours, holding the tin of cookies in her lap, until she's the last person in the waiting room. And then, finally, there he is, a strapping man in a sailor uniform.

I wiped my nose with my hand and pulled myself together, very briefly. "And after a while, she gives him the tin of his favorite cookies—she really labored over them; they're complicated cookies with a special design on top—and he says, 'Me bag is full to the brim,' and refuses to take them."

"Oh no," moaned one of my friends.

When Mrs. Hall and her son finally get to the rift that drove him away—these painful events with our children are rarely as tidy as a single explainable event, but this was TV—Mrs. Hall tells her son that she believed she was doing the right thing, turning him over to the police to help set him straight. "You broke me," her son replies as he strides to his train. Mrs. Hall runs beside him, saying, "I'm sorry, I'm sorry, I'm sorry," and when he gets on the moving train, he reaches through the window at the last minute and says he'll find room for the cookies after all.

"But she can't reach. And the cookies . . . the cookies . . . they smash to pieces on the platform!" I can't remember what dinner course we were on when I told this story. I hope I'd at least waited for dessert to cry all over the food. "And he's calling out the window, and she's running after the train, shouting, 'I can't hear you, son! I can't hear you son!'

"And—oh, wait, I forgot to tell you." I blew my nose into my napkin and looked around apologetically, because this was a big plot point. "There's been a deaf woman on the platform all along, serving tea. She's seen how sad Mrs. Hall is, and now this woman is running behind Mrs. Hall, and she's reading the son's lips. And after the train is gone from sight, this woman says to Mrs. Hall, 'Your son said, "I love you, Ma!"'"

I recently rewatched that episode—it's titled "Edward," the son's name—and cried all over again, even though by now my son and I were back in each other's lives. For the baby, at first. We'd meet at the Royal Ontario Museum on Sundays, hanging out in the children's play area or the sprawling wing of Buddha statues, which the baby seemed to identify with, staring silently at their smooth faces. Mary, who'd stayed in contact with her brother, started to join too. On one of the outings, I touched my chin with my hand and cut myself. "My God, Mom, you're bleeding!" Kelly said, and then Mary joined in, and they both walked me to the bathroom, one on either side, saying, "Mom! Are you okay?" I staunched the blood in front of the bathroom mirror, it really was gushing, and I'd never been so happy. Back in the play area, a small piece of toilet paper stuck to my chin, the baby stacked six wooden blocks into a small tower. "I did it," he said. It was his first sentence. It was perhaps a weight to put on one little boy's shoulders, to bring a family back together, but even though he was only two, he did it.

In the final scene of that *All Creatures* episode, Mrs. Hall and Siegfried, the often-difficult veterinarian, sit side by side in easy chairs so they don't have to look at each other as they talk about matters of the heart.

"I wish the past would invite me back to rectify a thing or two," he says.

"Oh, whatever it is, Mr. Farnon, you're forgiven."

I lost the navy pants I'd bought the day I saw my son on the subway platform. I hadn't taken them anywhere, so I knew they had to be in the house. Losing things was not uncommon for me, but usually the objects were transitional by nature: keys, glasses, gloves, umbrellas, and passports are most likely to be lost. But losing my pants *in my own house* felt more like losing my mind. For days, I searched upstairs and down. I sought help from experts on the internet. I imagined a quivering silver string from my chest to my pants, as one suggested. I imagined I *was* my pants, loung-ing rakishly in a dark corner sipping an old-fashioned. I consulted Gillian, the Buddhist gardener, whose experience of losing things was cosmic. Gillian had an astonishing memory for most things except misplaced objects. She described losing them as "a gap in time or missing time."

"It's interesting that your friend Gillian is a Buddhist." I'd called Nicole Anderson, that senior scientist at Baycrest in Toronto, who I sometimes spoke to about aging. "The Buddhism part is appropriate here because in a way losing something is not being present in the moment," she said. "It's kind of like the gap in time your friend described, because you stop paying attention. Losing things is almost always a failure of attention, not memory.

"Stress or trauma can also contribute to attention failure," Anderson added. "If you were experiencing any of that."

And there it was. I had become lost myself and so had lost my beloved new pants.

I didn't hide in my room during those bad days in my marriage. Kelly misremembered that part. But I made a room of my silence. It was Kelly who started to stay in his room. Keeping it tidy, keeping everything around him in order. On the subway platform, when I thought they were strangers, I was drawn to the little family's steady intent as they bundled their baby for the cold. But I think I had that wrong. I think I kept watching them because they seemed precarious. Their deliberation wasn't them being on top of the details; it was them holding on, with so much changed in their lives, when what I had wanted was for them to feel held on to. This was the fleeting glimpse I got of their precariousness. All the other times, when I'd known it was them, their happiness was what I saw. Or my own. But happiness goes by in a blur. The Florida orange, the orange pioneer hat, rushing trains, sliding doors.

When Kelly and Mary were children, I hadn't made a happy home. Or at least, the happiness from when they were little didn't last. Living together again with my son and his new baby was a chance for me to be the mother I might have been were it not for the steady thrum of misery with my husband. And for Kelly to show me how to create a happy family, how to do it properly. And he did do that. I'd never seen better parents than Kelly and Ivonne. But you don't get a redo, not really.

"Was it possible," said Tim the Jungian, "that losing your pants a couple of days after the domestic argument could have been an unconscious acknowledgment that you no longer wore the pants in the family?" And then, a new idea: "Perhaps you no longer want to wear the pants in the family?"

Eventually, I stopped searching for my pants. I reconciled myself to never seeing them again. A few weeks later, as I lay on my bed while the late-afternoon sun splayed across the room, a sudden thought made me sit up: my pants are in my ski bag.

This ski bag was something I kept at the ready, for the imaginary life I didn't lead, the one where I set out in the fresh white snow with the sun shining all around. I kept the bag handy, in my bedroom closet instead of down in the basement with the other sports stuff. When I unzipped it, there were my pants, sitting right on top with an untroubled air.

"A gap in time is a kind of bardo," said Tim at our next session. "A space between lives. A transition." I waited. "Your pants in the ski bag, and the freedom the bag represents, is a moment of defiance, perhaps, between the life you have and the life you imagine."

Dr. Anderson had given me two tricks for not losing things. "Do it, then say it" was the first one—as in, "I have put my pants in my ski bag." The second tip was "Say it *before* you do it." But what would I have said to my pants?

"Excellent blue pants. I'm still not sure why I'm about to zip you into my cross-country ski bag. Perhaps it's something to do with my family leaving, and it's time for me to set out too? To find that path that goes a bit farther than my backyard hut? Whatever the reason, I'm hopeful I'll find you again when I'm ready."

thirteen

OLD FRIEND, PART 3

THIS IS HOW IT BEGAN again.

I opened my eyes to an email from D. It was 7 a.m. My heart skipped a beat, not as romantic as it sounds when you're sixty-eight. But I missed D. And as much as I missed him, I missed the hopeful feeling he'd given me of changing my life, even when I hadn't expected or wanted to.

So I'd written one more time, to say that I'd seen Wim Wenders's *Perfect Days* and the main character had reminded me of him. It was a bit risky as a rejoinder because the character's job was cleaning toilets in Tokyo. But he was a lovely man. He had a bike, a camera, and a pleasing if slightly obsessive system for a modest and ordered life.

I now see much beauty in our walk. A day with moments of perfection. I added a link to a piano version of "Perfect Day," Lou Reed's 1972 song that might have been about dark need or might have been about romantic love. Both interpretations seemed to fit.

This 7 a.m. message was his response. I sat up in bed, put my phone in front of my face, and opened his email.

It was two photographs of Stalin.

The first was with Nikolai Yezhov, a good pal who oversaw Stalin's murderous purges. The second was the same photo except without Yezhov, after he'd fallen out of favor and Stalin disappeared him from the shot, an early example of a deepfake.

I admired the succinctness. I'd excised D after one meeting. I took his email as fair comment. It made me laugh too. I sprang out of bed and called Ellen. She didn't get the joke. "You're an insane dictator now? Don't reply to him."

All the way to Stalin? I replied immediately after I hung up with Ellen. He waited a day to write back.

Yes, Stalin. And living in the Annex.

I'd replayed our meeting many times before we got to Stalin. My first version was that D had been too intimate too fast, and that's what I'd run away from. But later I began to wonder if his all-in happiness to see me had startled me so badly because I was the one who was unavailable. Maybe I always had been. When I was seventeen, did I choose D, a boy I couldn't really have, to hold myself in reserve, that steady need to keep looking for the exits? And had I been doing the same thing ever since, choosing men whose emotional distance kept me at bay—which turned out to be a lovely, private, and safe inlet only I could reach?

I won't linger on the two hundred or so emails that followed, before we met again for the second time about two weeks later. But I will say to the romantic poets of the 1800s: thank God you didn't have email. It takes the hair-raising need and neediness of these situations and then collapses time, distance, and any semblance of reserve. At our age, I kept thinking, pointlessly, because the tempest of love is exactly the same at seventy as seventeen. The idea that love is kind, that it makes you sweet and happy, is also best put to rest. Between morning and night, D and I circled each other. It was more intimate than anything else we could have been doing. It was difficult to imagine how we would behave if we saw each other again.

I got in touch with my friend C, who was in her own messaging madness with a boy she'd fallen for when she was thirteen. Decades later, they were rekindling the affair, part of the second-chance love craze gripping boomers everywhere. Her first love was a doctor now too (what was it with these doctors?), and for C, going back was tied up with aging, "even though it wouldn't solve the problem of aging, or of not wanting to be the age I am."

"How often do you text?" I asked her.

"A lot," she replied.

"Like twenty a day?" I wanted to gauge her online jonesing against my own.

"More," she said. And then, wryly, because you're never sure who you're dating, no matter how well you knew them in the long-ago past: "He is not a mystery, but his sanity level may be."

D pointed me to the millions of internet search hits for studies on love vs. mania. One of them used MRIs to map the brains of people in love, showing that romantic love is not an emotion but a motivation system—an addiction—located at the base of the brain, right next to other drives, like hunger, thirst, and one more hit of cocaine. A Harvard study called "Love Actually: The Science behind Lust, Attraction and Companionship" described love as a kind of "total eclipse of the brain." Alexandra Molotkow wrote about the "limerence" effect for *Real Life* magazine. Rather than bringing two people together, limerence marks "the intrusive thoughts, the wild ups and downs triggered by your perception of their perception of you." Eclipse or limerence, our love mainlining might even have been making me and D sick, and who needed that with all the other ailments clamoring for seventy-somethings' attention?

Changes in love hormones could affect immune function, wrote D.

Ya, we need to get a grip.

We agreed to go for a walk along Lake Ontario on Easter Sunday. A day of resurrection, not crucifixion. No kissing or touching (Maria would be proud). Simply two people walking around getting to know each other, each familiar with our city, reclaiming it together—"deterritorializing it," was how D put it. That was something out of Deleuze. Something maybe D wanted to do to me. The night before, I lay in bed imagining how that would feel, to be unmapped and reclaimed. I felt dizzy even though I was lying down. Where was I now?

I sent him a photograph of an asparagus tart I'd made earlier that day. He sent me a photo of a swarm of larks.

D stood in front of his house, almost a straight shot south from my own house, me in midtown, him at the base of the city, before it hit the lake. He greeted me with a small wave. I did the same. This time I noticed the hard intelligence in his eyes and the soft wave of his hair. I noticed the fit of his blue button-down shirt.

"Would you like a tour before we head out?"

I entered a house that was as pristine as it was empty. Instead of feeling concerned over the lack of furniture, I felt calmed down. Stuff, and having too much of it, had begun to worry me. No such problem here. There was a gas fireplace, and there was a couch. It was a house whose minimal comfort offered something more private than soirées and dinner parties. No dining-room table, for starters.

"I took it down to the lath and then rebuilt it." D ran his rough hand along a smooth and true wall. "I throw myself into projects." He looked at me with the face I knew, his inquiring and restrained expression fully on me.

He led me into his kitchen—"central command"—and while he made us tea, I took in the order of his few things. Against one wall was the dark wood cabinetry he'd built; on the other, a large wooden desk with his computer. A couple of comfortable chairs. I was aware of the way D followed my reactions to everything he showed me, and I was aware of the pressure of his hand on my back, each finger its own power point, when he steered me onto his patio. We toured the garage, which housed his workshop, canoe, e-bike, and motorcycle. When we first started to email, he'd shown me pictures of him on the motorcycle in northern BC and the Yukon. "I'll never get on the back of a motorcycle," I'd said then. "When can we go for a ride?" I said now, imagining my arms around him, leaning into the curves of the road, my hair free on the wind. And just like that, my idea of romance rewired from candlelit dinners and hotels in Paris to motor-cycles and motels in Northern Ontario. I hadn't planned to upend the way I thought of my future, or known that I wanted something different from life. Or that life wanted something different from me.

"I had this idea last night," I said as D and I walked along the lake. He pulled my bag back up on my shoulder when it slipped down, as he had when I was seventeen, but otherwise kept his distance. My idea was that I would recreate every scene of our teenage courtship, all the things he didn't remember, to give him a kind of body recall. I'd imagined this moment on our walk, and how romantic it would be.

My story came out in a rush: "I sat beside you in that attic and you showed me the book you were reading, our knees were touching, we were maybe fourteen?" I was aware of my body bumping into him as the lake made a breeze on my face. "The night we all snuck out to the lake and stayed up to see the sunrise?" Meryl and I had cut holes in her mother's best blankets to wear as ponchos, which her mother never got over. "I remember falling asleep beside you wrapped tight in my blanket-poncho, you looking mystified. I guess I was fifteen?" I barely took a breath as I recited my list. "Sixteen, in my parents' den, and you took off my top but didn't touch me . . . In the field with the tall grass when the boy scouts went by single file—" I looked at D then and saw that he had the same rictus smile on his face that I'd had on our first walk, listening to me narrating a past he didn't remember. He had a theory, though: that the one who leaves forgets, and the one who's left remembers. After he told it to me, I tried and failed to recall details about men I had left.

"Besides, time doesn't work that way," he said. "The past doesn't stay the same. You can't replay it. It's like this cloud." We'd sat on a rock in front of the lake, Grimsby directly opposite, and he pointed to the clouds high and thin over the water. "*Cirrus uncinus* means curly hooks, also known as mares' tails. It means we're going to have a storm in the next forty-eight hours, at this place. So if you're traveling, you can say, 'It will rain here in forty-eight hours, but we won't be here then.'"

The wind was whipping up. We headed for a bar D knew, where he sat down on a velvet settee in the back room—bars have couches now, to make it seem like you're at home instead of going out—and gestured to me to sit beside him. We were on our third drink when he tucked my arm into his and tapped my bicep reflex just above my elbow, which tingled up my arm.

"Is that a doctor move?"

"Yes."

"Does it work?"

"Yes."

And then I was fully lit, and not only from the wine.

"Here we go," he said when I kissed him on the couch in a bar at 5 p.m. on Easter Sunday.

The next morning—after a lively public display, we'd each gone home alone, in small allegiance to our agreement not to touch each other—I woke up to a 4 a.m. email of various maps of the city: Garrison Creek and I don't know what else. Had I talked about my interest in maps? I wondered, groping for my glasses as I propped myself up in bed.

Sorry, maybe you're not interested in focusing on maps when you're having trouble focusing on anything. Thank you so much for coming out with me. I think we touched on some sensitive areas.

I replied that I had a sudden rash on my back (my sexy talk was out of practice, but I've always been rashy, and he was a doctor). He said he would need to fully examine me.

I love you like you don't even know, he said.

I'll bring you tea while you write, he added. Covering all the bases.

Forty-eight hours later, the rain did come—here, at this place—a huge, thunderous downpour in the middle of the afternoon, as I was working in my hut. Rain streamed through the new roof onto my head and my desk.

"The roof of my hut is leaking," I wrote to D. It felt like failure. It felt like nothing could ever work. It felt like imagining otherwise was folly. Best-laid plans. Leaks have this power. Something is entering where it should not, something becomes known even though you've built a roof to keep it out.

The third time I went to Laura's off-grid cabin on Johnson Lake, we called the guy who'd just built it because her new roof was leaking. This leak put us in a terrible way, like my leak in my hut. I saw my own fear in Laura's face as we sat in the dripping room waiting for the man to come. He was a working guy, handsome and certain about things, although he admitted to his own dark spiral about the leaking roof after he'd gotten our call. It turned out it was a minor issue, easily fixed, to the tremendous relief of us all. He'd brought his two daughters with him, Breezy and Amy, both under ten and white-blonde. I wrote their names on a piece of paper and kept it for years because names of sisters don't get better than that. When Breezy saw Laura's Kobo eReader, she asked what Laura was reading, and we talked about books until the roof repair was done.

"Dad, can we go to Long Beach?" Amy asked as he loaded up the truck.

"No, we'll go to Sleepy Cove."

"Why? The beach, Dad! The beach!" Amy and Breezy chanted at once.

"No." Dad did not explain his reason, which was relaxing for all of us. His non-negotiable position made it easier for the girls to accept his decision. They switched tacks.

"What's at Sleepy Cove, Dad?"

"The guy teaching lessons to the kids."

That seemed to do the trick. "Everyone happy as a clam in a shell," Laura said when they left, waving goodbye from the open windows of the pickup truck. We had each other, briefly, Laura, Cathrin, Amy, and Breezy. We had books, likely for all our lives. And we had a roof that no longer leaked.

"Leaks can be very frustrating," wrote D. He suggested I not think about the whole roof failing—*the sky is falling!*—but just a tiny point, which had been the situation on Laura's roof and likely was on my own, despite the puddles forming around me. "Sometimes the repair involves finding the leak on the inside with a probe, rather than recovering the outside." Which was what Laura's builder had done.

D proposed that instead of worrying, I go inside my house to get away from the splatting. So that's what I did. I switched locations. I changed where I was.

We put the Stalin days behind us. It was an abrupt shift in the world, a smash cut to a new direction.

Our meeting time was 3 p.m. "Three o'clock is always too late or too early for anything you want to do," said Sartre, which suited us. In his kitchen, we sat facing each other in comfortable chairs, our feet sharing the wooden footstool, often for hours. He continued to prepare a list each time we met—he disliked the "jazz improv" of random conversation— and then would give it to me once we had gone through each item. "Keep this, it's a good one." He also gave me small gifts: postcards, a key to his house, sage for burning, a few joints in an orange survival-match case with a quarter-sized mirror inside the cap. I held the mirror up to my face, preening. All I could see was my left eye.

"Pretty tiny mirror. Not much use for putting on lipstick in the wild."

"It's to make a flash to signal for help, Cathrin."

The best present was a doctor mallet to test my reflexes. "Don't overdo it," he said, "and let gravity do the work." Sometimes I put lipstick on with the tiny mirror while tapping my knee with the mallet, to my supreme pleasure.

I got to know the upstairs of his house. One double bed, two pillows, blue cotton sheets and quilt, and two stacks of clothes on a low, dark-wood shelf—one stack of about twenty identical jeans, the other of about twenty identical khaki green T-shirts.

"I see you like a green shirt."

"I like to wear the same thing every day." The blue button-down was him dressing up for me. "Your eyes are brown," he said later, repeating his most romantic line from when we were seventeen.

"Why do we love each other?" I said to his face very near my own.

"*Why* is the wrong question."

"Still," I quoted a sweet family TV show about grandparents I was streaming: "It's a gift for each of us to have someone to be kind to."

D moaned like I'd stabbed him in the face. "Stop trying to oppress me with your bright side," he said.

"Stop trying to convert me to your darkness." It was obvious we'd destroy each other as easily as we'd love each other. "No one is more capable of falsities nor as requiring of them than those who wish never to part ways." That's from *My Friends*,

Hisham Matar's book. My Old Friend and I were too different. "Too good to be true, too dangerous to be good," was how D put it. He poked at my safe and conventional midtown lifestyle, my carefully curated taste. I challenged his vocation as an isolate. My life was populous, his singular. He saw me tied to the needs of others. I watched him retreat into his privacy. We'd likely never exist in harmony. Harmony was not a place he desired to exist in, for one thing. "You want to please everyone, but we are pleased," he said. "We don't need you to please us." Sometimes we stepped away from each other, exhausted from giving too much or too little. So far, we'd come back. Although he still refused to put me on his motorcycle, erasing my fantasy version of us.

"Never," he said. "Too dangerous. We'll get you an e-bike instead."

"Never," I said. "Too fast."

His bandwidth for me or anyone else was about an inch wide. Mine, with my grandson, family, friends, and writing every day in the hut, was about the same. Our meetings were well spaced but like a heroic poem when they happened. And then we went home to our own beds at 10 p.m. because we both wanted a good night's sleep.

"I had a kind of vision as a child." D was lying beside me in my bed for a change. "Why are there so many pillows?" He flung several onto the floor like a kid rooting through a toy box. "And why are they all so thin?"

"I like a thin pillow," I said. I was propped on my elbow, looking into his face, when he sat up suddenly and took me by my shoulders and then positioned me on my back beside him, so we were both talking up to the ceiling, holding hands.

"Is that a psychiatrist move?" I said as I relaxed beside him.

"It's good to have something else to look at when you talk," he said, and then continued the story of his childhood vision. "Maybe I was nine or so, and I was driving with my dad on a country road with ridges and deep valleys and sensing the scenery as what one's life could look like when seen from a distance. I remember having this rare feeling of your whole life laid out in front of you without any clue about the details."

His words traveled up to the ceiling and then flowed back down on me, like water in a fountain. We were flows for each other, D said.

"I realized for the first time on that drive through that landscape that time is space, like on a map. Because the only way we see time is through changes in space, right? Like the rotations of the earth."

I remembered Saman at the McMaster Library saying that place is just space with meaning. "I've had this idea for a long time," I said to the ceiling after a bit. It was a slow talk. "To walk west on Bloor Street and never stop. Just walk and walk."

"We'll become nomad partners together." He would follow me away from what he called my over-coded life. And then, wildly seductively: "It would be good for your writing."

The next morning, I composed a love note for D, who'd gone home to his own bed at 10 p.m. Before I hit send, an email landed from him. It was a picture of lint. "Lint is an anti-fabric. Where you see a dust bunny, the dust mite sees a palace with many rooms." *Your eyes are brown. Lint is a mite palace.* His love talk hadn't changed in fifty years, and it was as potent for me at seventy as it had been at seventeen. If love is being hooked on another human being, it follows that the first dose becomes the model for understanding all love that follows. D and I were never going to be a romantic comedy. "I don't want to get old with you," he said. "But I will get imperceptibly older with you."

"It's Aunt Mary and Don all over again," said Laura. I was on a three-way call with my sisters that Ann had set up from Vancouver and was surprised I'd forgotten the late-life romance of my mother's oldest sister. Don was the boy Mary had loved at seventeen, and he came back into her life in her sixties, after her husband died. Like me and D, they'd never lived more than a few blocks apart, in St. Catharines. "Don told me the outside package had changed, but inside I'm still the same Mary," our aunt had said to me and Laura when she revealed her romance, the life of the girl in the woman. When Don got cancer fifteen years later, she didn't visit him in the hospital any more than she had her husband—she disliked sick beds and took to her own only briefly before she died. But she was bereft when he departed.

"They played footsie at my wedding," the image came back to me on our call. "I remember thinking at the time that they couldn't possibly be having sex at their age." Ann—in love again herself, after her separation, with a jazz saxophone player named Saul—laughed happily. Me and D, Ellen and her D, Ann and Saul, Mary and Don, D's mother and the man she lived with for fifteen years until his death. "I guess he was the love of her life," said D.

"I guess you have to see this through," said Meryl. She was the first person I'd called about D, after he sent me his Old Friend email. She'd known me at seventeen, when I'd fallen for him. And she knew me fifty years later, when she watched me fall for him all over again. She wasn't going to get carried away, for my sake.

"I guess I do," I said.

fourteen

MOVING UP AND MOVING OUT

"WE PLAYED A GUESSING GAME about how many ladders you have, Tim."

I was sitting between my brothers, Tim and David, one on either side of me on their big and comfortable couch. Tim had started to nod off, and this ladder thing barely woke him up. "What number did you guess?"

"Six," I said. "Laura guessed eight. So Nancy said, 'Add them together.' That's fourteen ladders, Tim."

"Wait, that's not all," David jumped in. "Guess what we found in the barn when we arrived?"

My brothers had finally moved into their new home, the one Sam had located on my map of St. Catharines at the birthday party, back when it was little more than an idea of a future. Now here it stood, on four acres in Fonthill, also known as the short hills of Niagara, very near to St. Catharines. Their low-slung house—the single level that faced the quiet country road expanded to two broad-viewed stories in the back—was set into one of the hills that sloped west into a verdant hollow. I called it the Commune because it seemed like a modern twist on the back-to-the-land movement of our youth. Tim had been part of that movement more than fifty years earlier, on one of British Columbia's Gulf Islands. There'd been sixty people living on that commune in 1970, with a father figure at the head (make of that what you will).

"This time, no one's in charge, and we're working it out as we go, but it's still an unconventional way to live," he said. Less and less: multigenerational households are the fastest-growing type in Canada. I'd tried it myself, for those eighteen months with my son and his family. I didn't know it then, but we were part of a movement to reclaim a way of living that's never been left behind by many rural, northern, and newly arrived Canadians. Sprawling multigenerational setups designed to invite people in, instead of nuclear-family units that keep people out.

I was a frequent visitor, setting out with whoever had wheels; the trips merged into each other. This one was at the back end of the building push, in late spring. The work pace had slowed, and naps were back on the agenda. Everyone else had gone for a pre-lunch walk in a drizzling rain, but Tim and David and I stayed behind.

"We found two more ladders in the barn when we moved here," said David. "And they're better than any of the ladders Tim has."

"Tim, why do you have so many ladders?"

Tim closed his eyes again beside me. "Of all the sins you could have, it seems to me the sin of too many ladders is a lesser one."

David jumped up to get his laptop. "I want to show you the beehives I'm ordering. It's a less invasive way to get honey." On the big couch, David flipped through pictures of stylish wood-frame beehouses, the kind of tidy setup I'd like to move into myself in my downscaling years. "Instead of scraping the honey, you pour it out the spigot."

"Friends of mine order their bees from Italy," I said. "They come by airplane, frozen or hibernating or something?" I'd exhausted the total of my bee-transport knowledge. "Apparently, Italian bees are quite angry."

Tim stirred but kept his eyes closed. "There will be no bees from Italy."

David cast his arm across our view. A tall meadow of clover, asters, daisies, and goldenrod quivered in the morning rain. He planned to add cardinal flowers and meadow blazing stars, with red and pink blooms as showy as their names and hard for a bee to miss. "Our bees will come," he said. "This is a bee paradise."

I was pretty sure he was right. Even by my small measure of paradise—that it would always smell sweet and birds would sing every day—the Commune ticked those off. When there are so many locations that could be anywhere—the strip malls and big-box stores with "no there there," as Gertrude Stein said sweepingly about California—you want to pay attention when you land somewhere. Place is space with meaning, said Saman, the map curator. This small community of people who chose to live together with nature all around seemed to have found their place. To put it another way, each time I visited the Commune, it seemed like an answer to my question, or at least *one* answer: Where are we now?

I wasn't the only one who thought so.

Laura took the elevator to the twenty-second-floor apartment she'd soon be moving into. She'd never lived high. She was holding a box with a shower curtain, wineglasses, and half a dozen flower vases. "Just a few necessities," she'd called me, laughing. The elevator door opened to a man wearing a toolbelt. Laura and I love a man with a toolbelt.

"Sell your house to come here?" he said.

"Yes," said Laura. She'd sold the beloved house that had been a haven to her and me and to anyone passing through in need of warmth and comfort.

"The first thing I said to the new owner of my house was 'How do you do? Here's the snow shovel,'" said the man on the elevator.

"Take my rake!" said Laura.

"It's always some man on the elevator, coming and going to the parking garage," Laura told me after she'd dropped off her necessities. "They're all, 'This is the best place you could ever live.' Like Dad. It makes me feel at home."

"That's nice." I smiled wanly.

"This change is very hard on me," I said about Laura's decision to move to anyone who would listen. Her status as my older sister meant that I watched what she did and then emulated it. When she went on birth control at eighteen, she helped me do the same when I turned seventeen. When she discovered Margaret Atwood and Alice Munro and Margaret Laurence, so did I. She was the first in our family to graduate from university; eight years later, I was the second. She became a lawyer to fight for justice; I became a journalist for the same reason. Now she was shedding The House. There, I could not follow her.

Those months when she'd dropped off plastic pumpkins and lawn chairs and wooden salad bowls were the prelude; I just hadn't known to what. The Swedish call the process of culling a life's accumulation of things *döstädning*. At my retirement party, Laura kept gleefully telling people, "I have to get back to my death cleaning!" To my vast alarm. We had a pact to stay on top of each other's hair dye to the end. It was easier than talking about our own mortality, or the unthinkable prospect of being left behind.

Laura's move up, into the high-rise, happened around the same time my brothers moved out, to the Commune. One day she'd said she'd be carried out of her house feet first, and the next she'd landed on the twenty-second floor, or that's how it seemed to me. My brothers were part of the intergenerational-living movement. Laura had joined the boomer movement out of single-family homes and into apartment buildings, there to meet other people who valued their autonomy and independence.

"No stairs," Laura answered when I asked how she could disrupt my life this way. I was getting my first tour of the graciously large and still-empty apartment. "No maintenance. No worries. I turn the key in the door, and I don't have to think about one single thing." The subway (with elevator), grocery store, pharmacy, liquor store, and a well-stocked independent bookstore were all within a three-minute walk; she'd timed them before she moved. Can't open a jar? Can't change a light bulb? There was always going to be someone nearby who could.

"I remember Dad saying when they moved to their condo that he could take the elevator straight to his car in the basement, and I thought, Just shoot me now. But you know what? That turns out to be totally great." She looked down at her fluffy dog, Buddy, standing at our feet on the sweep of balcony that overlooked the city. "Best of all, the ravine is just out the door, and Buddy and I love that, don't we, Buddy?" He gave his tail a single wag. He looked as uncertain as me.

It was a lot of change in one year. I felt like one of the timorous fathers in a Jane Austen novel when a daughter announced plans to move a few hundred feet across the flowering meadow to live with her new husband. I could hear my voice wobble when I tried to discuss this plan of Laura's, even though her new apartment was only a twenty-minute walk away.

By now it should not have been a surprise that the older siblings were spryer with change than the younger, more as time passed. "We were a different generation than you and Ann," Laura said. "Dad had two jobs when we were young. There was a lot of hustle, a sense you needed to go forward. They were more settled by the time you came." In the last couple of years, Laura had replaced both her hips, had surgery on each wrist, bought an off-grid cabin on a northern lake, and set out at the slimmest urging to Sicily or wherever her springy titanium joints would take her. Now this apartment. If the question of age was one of location more than identity, Laura's new digs were a clear-eyed response.

Ann was more like me, doing everything she could to keep her home, post-divorce.

She'd gone the farthest away to live, to East Vancouver. Her house was on a hill, with four sides of windows like my own, and surrounded by lush and leafy West Coast plants in every shade of green. I'd felt vulnerable living in my house after my divorce. One year separated, Ann used the word "precarity" about her place.

"Home is a tender spot for me," she said tenderly. I still thought of Ann as my little sister and felt protective (forget the poking now). I'd ferociously pulled her out of a circle of taunting kids when I was in eighth grade, Ann in first. "You were so mad at me," Ann said recently. "Mad at *you*?" It was astonishing how we could carry the wrong stick our whole lives for want of a simple conversation that would set us straight. "I was furious with the other kids for scaring you. I wanted to obliterate them."

Ann reminded me that our parents sold our childhood home on Nelles Boulevard in Grimsby—the one where we'd found the secret passageway—when she was still in her final year of high school. "I sat in the empty house on moving day and was bereft." But she wasn't allowed to talk about her own loss of place. "Mom had made herself very fragile around the move," back to St. Catharines, where she was born and where her sisters had remained. I squirmed slightly on Ann's kitchen stool. I had some experience making my child's crisis about myself. "We never had the words to help each other."

"Finally, in this house, I feel like I'm home again," Ann told me as the rain came down outside the open kitchen door, the kind of steady background rain that can make a conversation feel intimate. "The way light streams in from a window, the way the air flows through, the space for thought, the room for friends. Simple, everyday things. Without them I feel off balance."

Ann got up to pour us more wine, then leaned her elbows on the other side of the counter to face me. Her eyes were bright. "I feel fierce about staying in place. In this place." She went through her list of how she hoped to keep her house for her and her daughters, now that her partner had left. "I could renovate the basement and live there so the girls could live upstairs," she told me. "Or I could sell the basement flat to fund the mortgage. Or rent the whole house and bank the money for a while."

"Ann," I interrupted. "Your decision to stay here is full of energy."

"Or maybe I'll take in boarders like you have," she continued.

"Being here means continually thinking about what 'here' means to you," I said.

"But I'm not so keen on boarders."

Neither of us was listening, but we were in the flow of each other's hopes and worries. We would keep our houses too, though for how long, we didn't know.

"The word I keep saying to myself is 'relief,'" said Laura. We were sitting on the couch in her now-furnished apartment. All that culling had been smart, and not just for the people she wanted to spare the job of going through her things. Her new home had all the warmth of her old one, but it wasn't overstuffed with her past. It was modern and sleekly streamlined. It looked forward instead of back.

"It's time," Laura said, and I followed her to her balcony. We stood side by side as the setting sun lit the tall, narrow buildings to our west like candles on a cake. It felt like a celebration.

"You're exactly where you should be," I said to Laura. I meant it, finally.

"I found my ground," she said. It seemed like a funny thing to say twenty-two stories up, but I understood. She'd hated to lose the vibrant community of the people on her street, but if you believe in community, you find it wherever you are. Not only that, she was living in a place she could come and go from with ease and hoped never to face an old-age home.

"Here they come! Look!" Laura pointed over our heads. This was what we were on the balcony to see. Two red-tailed hawks curved in the evening sky, closer, then farther. It was an unrestrained, masterful feeling, being up there with the birds. To be one of them. Imagine! "They come up from the ravine every night about this time." The sunset wind was rising, blowing our hair high. "I think it's Mom and Dad, welcoming me home."

On the elevator down, as I headed out and Laura took Buddy for a last spin of the day, I asked the question that had been on my mind. I wondered if the same impulse to leave my house would come over me when I got to my mid-seventies.

"How do you know when it's the right time to move?"

"You just know."

"Like when I retired? How that came over me?"

"Yes, like that."

After we said goodnight, a lively man, older than her, joined her on the up elevator.

"What floor are you going to?" he asked.

"Twenty-two," said Laura.

"I'm nineteen. You're closer to God than I am."

"It would take more than that," Laura said.

He laughed and waved goodbye. "I'll see you around."

"I'm seventy-five." Tim stood in front of a row of stakes, where he envisioned sweet and sour cherry trees, apple, plum, peach, pear, even an apricot.

"I disapprove of the apricot," I said. I'd seen every kind of fruit tree growing up but never an apricot.

"Fruit trees take three years to bear fruit, so I say we get planting."

"Tim has started to put 'I'm seventy-five' in front of every sentence, as if he's going to be dead any minute." Nancy gave him a worried look; she was eleven years younger. (Tim did marry the girl next door, but she was in a cradle the first time they met, went the jokes on their wedding day.)

"Pure manipulation. I just want my fruit trees," said Tim. My brothers and I had joined the after-lunch walk now that the rain had stopped. "I use any weapon in my arsenal."

"I think there are things you can only learn best, or finally, later in life." I'd asked my brothers what they thought about their seventies, with mine just ahead of me, and this was Tim's reply. "Before we decided to move here, I looked ahead to what our lives would be in twenty years." We'd left the imaginary fruit trees, with their imaginary blossoms filling my head. "I saw David living alone in his bachelor apartment. And me and Nancy banging around in our house. I wanted our lives to open up, not close in more and more until we were alone in a tiny room."

"Everybody ends up alone in a tiny room, though," I said. "The final room. Like Mom and Dad."

"Let's keep that final-room stay as brief as possible," said Tim, echoing Laura's outlook.

"I don't think about what's coming." David opened the mesh gate of the newly planted vegetable garden, long and narrow to keep out the deer; they dislike confined spaces. The tomatoes were a no-go. But the raspberries and radishes were up, with beans, squashes, and lettuces to come, each hopeful row neatly labeled.

"You're kind of on borrowed time, though, aren't you, Dave?" said Nancy. "It's a miracle you're here with us." David had had his own rough patch—a fifty-year one—with alcohol addiction.

"I remember the past." David turned to look at Nancy in the garden. This was not his favorite subject, but he faced it. "The remembering makes sure that I don't do it again." He picked a few raspberries and handed them around, sweet as candy. "I live in the moment. Not what I'll do in the next twenty years, but this week."

Tim seized the moment. "Like plant fruit trees."

Local bees and butterflies landed and lifted on flower helipads as we passed through the meadow at the center of the property to the row of deciduous trees at the back. The dawn redwood was twenty-five feet wide, with bark like a deep-brown undulating sea. It was an ancient tree, almost extinct in the 1940s. "They call it the reemergence of a living fossil," David said.

"What's this one again?" The tall, twisted tree looked like it would murder me if I got too close, which I did not. It had spikes.

"Shagbark hickory," said David. "It's basically a locust tree with thorns, and it dates to the time of the dinosaur. Now the thorns have mostly been bred out." The black walnut was maybe 150 years old. If I were doing a focus group on aging, I was in the right place.

Sometimes, standing somewhere, I've felt a tug. The first time was when an Indigenous guide took my husband and me to what he described as a "power spot" in a hidden ravine on the north shore of Lake Superior, and my knees almost buckled from the force of it. The second tug came up through the sidewalk at the intersection of Wall Street and Broadway in New York, when it seemed that place was the center of the financial universe because of the power of the location, and not from all the moneymaking. More recently, I was walking with my friend Jason in his west-end Toronto neighborhood when the streets dipped. "I got this feeling," I wrote to him afterward, "that it was a power spot." Jason agreed. "It's the echo of a ghost creek." Jason was working on a project to map some of the buried waterways of the city, and he also made ink from acorns or bits of rusted metal that he foraged on the streets. Neither of us was shy around magical thinking. "It does seem kind of dreamlike?" he wrote back. "Important somehow."

Rupert Sheldrake is a British biologist and author once spurned by mainstream science for his theory of "morphic resonance." Sheldrake's idea—that memory is inherent in nature, and that trees together were greater than any one tree, connected and communicating at the root—was easy to hold on to as I stood in the middle of the Commune's old-growth trees. (Sheldrake said families have morphic resonance too, with a system of collective memory connecting members of a close group even when they are many miles apart.) What was scoffed at in the 1980s is mainstream now. Trees cooperate and nurture in lives not that different from our own in *Finding the Mother Tree*, by Canadian Suzanne Simard, and *The Hidden Life of Trees*, by German Peter Wohlleben—both bestsellers and respected (enough) by science. Taking this a step further, Ferris Jabr's 2024 book, *Becoming Earth: How Our Planet Came to Life*, reported that earth's interior is not barren but full of dense rock-breathing microbes: that is, life doesn't happen on top of earth; the earth itself is alive. It's a kind of return to the Gaia (Mother Earth, literally) hypothesis of the 1960s environmental movement.

"It's the power of nature," David said as he leaned both hands on his tall walking stick among the trees. "The flora and the fauna. It gives you a feeling of well-being."

"I'd rather not put it into words," said Tim.

At the end of the walk, and of the day, when it was time to leave, I bent over my aqua-blue Converses, tying the laces with moderate difficulty.

"This is why people our age use slip-on shoes, Cathrin." Tim was part of the pileup at the door behind me. "This is why shoelaces will soon be obsolete."

"No one needs more than two colors of Converses," said David. "There's your white and there's your black." Whatever would I do without their steady tutelage?

Nick, Sam's cousin on Nancy's side, would be the one to drive me home that night. His car was from Japan and had the steering wheel on the right, so I kept feeling like I was in a driverless car—an innovation I impatiently awaited to change my life. Nick was drawn to the Commune too. He came as often as he could, between treatments for the pernicious cancer that had taken hold a year earlier, when he'd turned thirty-five. He liked to sit with Tim and David outside under the towering trees and listen to them talk, Nick told me on the drive home along the darkening QEW. The smoke from Tim's cigar would curl toward the half-moon as the fireflies came up luminous in the night.

"Please don't tell me they got onto the Roman Empire?" I told Nick how they'd quizzed me one morning when they were renovating my tiny bathroom during Covid. It was 7 a.m. at the time. It was always something with my brothers.

"They talked about fission the other night," Nick said. "Dave asked me what I knew about the Large Hadron Collider. I can't get enough of those guys."

Tim did find the words for what he experienced around the trees. "It's a feeling of goodness," he called to tell me. "They shelter each other, and us as well. They are our hosts, not the other way around. That's the real commune."

"That's nice," I said. "Maybe your love of ladders is connected to your love of trees. I mean, they're both high and you can climb them. Swaying in the top. Trees, ladders—they're a lot alike, when you think of it."

"That's a stretch," said Tim.

fifteen

THE STORY OF THE WOLF

THERE IS ONE STORY I haven't told yet from our walk around the Commune. It was after we'd passed the old-growth trees and come out to a clearing on a grassy mound. There, a group of us stood in a loose circle. Or it might have been on another walk, on another afternoon, with some other people, at the same spot. As I said, the trips to the Commune merged. Let's put all of us together, in the clearing on the afternoon the sun came out, when I said to my nephew, "Tell us the story of the wolf, Sam."

Sam was a good storyteller. He had pacing and humor, but more importantly, he understood what made a story one that he wanted to tell. That often meant it arced up. Sam first told me the story of the wolf in the road when he was building my hut. He described how he'd driven his sick cousin, Nick—Nick and Sam were born thirty-six years earlier, two months apart, and had been cousin-brothers ever since—across the country, to bring him home for urgent cancer care.

People often tell stories of animals helping them through grief and suffering. One good friend said his father returned every spring as the same robin, another that her friend arrived as a red cardinal after he suddenly died. Laura believed the hawks were Mom and Dad come back to watch over her in her new home. So I accepted Sam's story of a wolf appearing to his very ill cousin as an optimistic story, even a supernatural one. And it was just the same when Sam told the story the second time, at my urging, on that grassy clearing. By the end, it felt like we'd all been part of a virtuous circle where goodness and happiness prevailed.

I thought about Nick often, after the first and second tellings of the wolf story. I didn't know Nick as well as Sam, since he was from the other side of Sam's family, but he was a person you met and then wanted to meet again as soon as possible. That night he drove me home from the Commune in his Japanese car with the steering on the right, he talked about what the place meant to him. "I've had a lot of thoughts and ideas come to me since my diagnosis," he said. "And I've learned not to doubt any of it. More and more, I have a feeling of awakening to myself when I come to the Commune."

So when I returned to the Commune to ask Sam for a third telling, wanting to write it down, I'd hoped Nick would be there. He was too unwell, but I didn't know that when I asked Sam for the story one more time. "My heart sank when you asked him," Nancy said to me later. "I wasn't sure what Sam would do."

It took some time for Sam to say to me, privately and grim-faced, "Okay, let's do this." I followed him through various rooms, many newly built, until we found a quiet place on the lower level. Tim was there, watching a baseball game. When Sam and I sat and faced each other across a small table, Tim turned the sound off but kept his eyes on the TV. He'd listen, and I think that's why Sam chose this room. There were plenty of empty ones. He wanted his father nearby.

"This was never a story about Nick being cured," Sam began. And then I knew he would not be, and I understood the burden I had put on my nephew. "That's not what the story of the wolf is about."

Nick had been away for many years, in Australia, Japan, and Banff, Alberta. When he became ill, he called Sam from Banff. "I've been traveling for so long, Sam," he said. "I feel like this diagnosis is the final sign to come back." Sam got on the first plane, to drive his cousin home.

"As we drove, we talked about a picture of a wolf that hung in our room at our gramps' house when we were kids."

During his previous tellings, Sam had stood and often waved his arms in front of him for emphasis. Now he sat still. The only sound outside of his voice was the wind in the trees, like a low song.

"It was always this photo we talked about because it wasn't what you'd expect to see in the bedroom of a child." Sam scrolled on his phone and then showed me a picture of a wolf in the wild. Half of its face was hidden behind a birch tree, so the wolf was peering out with one amber eye looking right at you. It was a vivid portrait, as intimate as it was frightening.

"I can see why it stood out to you," I said, handing the phone back. When Nick and Sam's grandparents died, it was Sam who brought the photograph to his parents' cottage in Northern Ontario. It hung over Tim and Nancy's bed.

"So we're talking about this picture, and we're bringing Nick home," Sam said. There was a lot to think about on the drive. Nick had made himself a special seat in the back, for the pain, but they still had to make frequent stops to let him move around. They couldn't eat fast food because of the cancer. "I'm googling all the time where to eat, where to eat, looking for family places with homemade food," said Sam. "We got as far as Winnipeg. The next morning, Nick said, 'Let's make a push for Ontario. Let's get to Sault Ste. Marie.'"

Sam tapped on his phone across the table from me for a moment, then looked up. "That was about thirteen hours away.

"I said, 'Okay, Nick, here we go. We can do this push.' I'm a good driver, but I'm white-knuckling because of Nick's right-side car from Japan." Sam googled a family restaurant called the Log Cabin, the first suitable place to eat in Ontario. "I think it's going to be a little backwoods cabin, but there are dozens of cars. They ask if we have a reservation, but they get us a table anyway and we have a great meal."

Tim, at the mention of food, reached for a bowl of chips. (I have the same Pavlovian response when someone says "Chablis.") His eyes stayed on the screen, and he remained silent but his willingness to let words rest helped the story land how it chose.

Nick went for a walk after each meal, and Sam hadn't yet received the bill when he came back and said, "I'm pretty sure I just saw a wolf." "You don't see wolves this close," the server told them. "Show me where you saw this wolf," Sam said to his cousin, so Nick took him to the edge of the crowded parking lot.

"He was over there, about twenty feet, not even," Nick said. "I thought it was a deer and then realized, That's not a deer, that's a wolf. He was looking right at me and then walked away."

"I believe you, man."

Sam paused, telling me the story, and wiped his eyes. "Talking about the wolf was an emotional conversation for Nicky and me. We knew right away it was our gramps looking out for us."

I forced myself not to look down or away. I'd made him do this. I wasn't going to abandon him now.

Back in the car, Sam told me, it got dark quickly. Half an hour later, the fog came up. "It was really foggy, a thick fog. So now I'm driving on the right side of the car on a two-lane Northern Ontario highway with transport trucks flying past in the foggy dark.

"What happened next was a deer walked out of the fog and right in front of us. We stopped about five feet away—it was a good thing I was driving slowly—and then I saw that it wasn't a deer. It was a wolf. In the middle of the road."

Usually, at this point in the story, Sam would have a look of awe on his face. This time he was matter-of-fact. "The wolf walked in front of the car. Not rushing, not flinching, not fazed. It just stood there, peering into the window." Sam and Nick and the wolf all looked at each other, Sam wasn't sure for how long. "This was not any wolf, Aunt Cathrin. This was a majestic wolf." Like in the picture, he didn't say. "We slowly drove past it in dead silence. I think we were silent for three minutes as we drove away." Nick in the back seat found a picture online and passed it up to Sam. "A wolf is absolutely what we saw," Nick said. "They don't live around here, so I don't even know . . . "

"And then we were both crying," said Sam. He cried now, and so did I. The wind song in the trees was louder outside at the end of the afternoon.

"But the story doesn't end there," Sam said, and I remembered that it didn't. "When we got back home, I told my brother Conor about the wolf, and he said, 'Wait, Sam. There's more to this story.'" As a small child, Conor was so frightened of the wolf over the bed at his grandparents' house that he called out one night. His grandfather sat beside him on the bed and said, "Conor, you're looking at this all wrong. That wolf isn't there to hurt you. He's there to protect you. You're part of his pack. That's why he's here, over the bed."

Sam stopped talking.

"It's a story about giving Nick the strength to beat the cancer," said Tim, turning to us. Sam might have agreed in the first two tellings, but not this time.

"I never thought the wolf was there to make Nick better," Sam said to his father. "Nick didn't think so either. The wolf was there to tell him that wherever he goes, the wolf is looking out for him. I understand that 'wherever' isn't necessarily here with us." Sam was calm now. "But I like to think that there's a wolf pack waiting for him. And that I'll see him again in the wolf pack."

"Can I see the picture one more time, Sam?" I studied the wolf. Now that the delightful story had become a mournful one, I thought about my own need to find the bright side in most things. It was me as much as Sam who wanted every story to arc up.

—

"Well, the name of your first book was *The Bright Side*," Ellen said, on another walk with her dog, Sally. The walking conversations I've related so far, about divorce and our mothers in heaven and old boyfriends with the same name, might give the wrong idea of the general tenor of our talks. Mostly we chatted endlessly about how Pluto in Aquarius was going to mess with our hairdos. Or how we'd disburse our winnings when we won the $60 million lottery. "I'll give you enough to pay off your mortgage," Ellen said. "How about round it up to a million?" I countered. "You've got sixty, after all." "Do you want to pay off your mortgage, or don't you?" We could both get pretty steamed about the division of our imaginary assets and would strike ungrateful imaginary recipients from the list, including each other. Our favorite conversation, though, was about the perfect way to boil an egg. We were famous, in fact, for our boiled-egg conversations, ever since Kelly—who'd listened for some time to our comparisons of the merits of the three- versus four-minute egg—had slowly banged his head on the dining room table. He was a teenager at the time. Whenever we wanted a private conversation after that, Ellen would say, "Start the egg in just one inch of water," and Kelly would flee the room with his hands over his ears.

"But there was an undercurrent of fear that ran through that whole book," Ellen said. And more fear since, I thought but didn't say, as we headed into the last quarter, with death creeping into every thought. "Where do you put the hard part? Where do you put the fear?" Ellen seemed to want an answer.

"You Vanstone it," I said. It was her family name, but also the term she used for putting your head down and pushing through, no matter what.

We paused at the last stoplight before the dog park. There were twelve seconds left to cross. We agreed to wait for the next green. "You fear death much more than I do," she said as we watched the seconds flash by. This statement surprised me, in ways I could hardly say to myself, let alone to Ellen.

Ellen had told me she had cancer almost two years earlier, on a phone call from Winnipeg, where she had moved to write and visit her family. I was working in my hut when my phone rang, and she began without preamble. "A dumb lump has been diagnosed as Stage 4 cancer." She was astonished and angry. The news encased me. But I moved almost immediately to practicalities. She didn't want emotion any more than I did. How fast could she get back to Toronto for the right care? How could Sally get home with her? No option would be fast enough for my liking.

Her brother drove her from Winnipeg to Toronto, with Sally in the back seat, just as Sam drove Nick. Very quickly, she began immunotherapy treatment for the tumors and lesions all over various organs, with limited success. Adding insult to injury, as Ellen put it, the treatment also left her with permanent adverse effects. She agreed to move on to a series of immunotherapy research trials to slow the progression of her cancer, and more heroically—I don't use the term lightly—to help to slow the growth of future cancers in other patients. Immunotherapy sounds nicer than chemotherapy. But it's brutal. It activates the immune system to stamp out the cancer, and in so doing creates other autoimmune diseases, like rheumatoid arthritis, diabetes, and colitis. Today's advances in cancer research are almost beyond imagination, but so is the individual toll on the patients like Ellen who help make them possible.

These medical assaults, we could talk about. Ellen being so sick she might not be here? That we could not talk about. I'd avoided the subject, I thought, to protect her. But I was really protecting myself from the idea of losing Ellen. That's probably also why I haven't written about it here until now.

As we crossed the street and headed for the dog park, I told Ellen that in my book, she wasn't sick.

"What? Why on earth?"

"I want you to be healthy on these pages." I bent my head, trying to Vanstone my grief.

"I want you to write about me as I am." She took Sally off leash, which meant Sally sat tall and calm beside us. "I used to think, if something went wrong, 'Just off me now,'" Ellen said.

I reminded her of the time we saw the French film *Amour,* and the old woman poured the tea on the table instead of into her cup. We were both horrified. "When we left the movie theatre, you asked if I'd help you die if it ever came to that."

"What'd you say?"

"I said no."

That was twelve years ago. We weren't yet sixty. We'd laughed then about where you drew the line: a niggling cough, a twisted ankle, one more hemorrhoid on the already overcrowded encampment. But the line retreats the nearer you get to it. I once came close to hitting a woman at a gallery opening when she insisted she would never submit to treatment for a serious cancer. "You have no idea until you're in that situation yourself," I kept repeating. *Only the living talk about how they'll die; the dying talk about how they'll live*—I'd heard a doctor say that once.

"You don't fear death?" I asked my friend at last. Ellen had only very recently begun to say out loud that her illness was *incurable*. I was with her at Princess Margaret hospital when the doctor leaned in to sympathetically say those exact words to Ellen's face: "Your cancer is incurable." When the appointment was over, we almost ran to Queen's Park, nearby, where we started to cry under a linden tree. "It's the worst possible news," said Ellen, and we held hands. And then neither of us talked about it again for a year-and-a-half. She had an elaborate system of subterfuges to describe her illness in a less dire way to anyone who asked, and after a while I almost bought into the story. This was the first time she'd said incurable since that day at Princess Margaret. It was like a light being turned off and having to feel your way in the dark.

"Depends on the day," Ellen answered my question. Sally suddenly lunged at a man gliding by on a skateboard and then chased him around the park, barking like a hound of hell. I have also neglected to mention that Sally had two sides. The skateboard man was not happy, he let us know, after Ellen finally lured Sally back with a treat. "Bad girl," she said, patting Sally's head and giving her another liver biscuit.

Ellen looked at me beside her on the park bench. "You're dying too," she said, not unkindly. "I just happen to have more information about that event than you do. We're all dying all the time."

"Tim the Jungian once said something similar."

Around the time of these conversations about death and dying, I'd traveled with a group of friends to Gillian and her husband Ron's cabin in the woods in the Eastern Townships of Quebec. I did this while rereading *The Lord of the Rings* trilogy, retreating into a familiar fantasy. At the cabin, a stream ran past the door, and a woodland path beside the stream led to a cool pond. It was like living in the happy Shire while reading about the happy Shire. Over dinner, I'd describe what was going on with the elves and the hobbits, to the agony of my companions. ("Not another fucking elf," one of them quoted C.S. Lewis, Tolkien's friend and rival.) Undaunted, I filled my fork with arugula and said: "Frodo just told his friends he'd carry the ring, 'though I do not know the way.'" My voice caught and my eyes filled with tears. "What is *going on* with you?" one of my pals asked, mystified and bored at the same time.

I've thought about that question. You can't have the happy Shire without the doom of Mordor. Finally accepting that was what was going on with me meant letting go of an enemy I'd held on to my whole life. Being alive meant being in a battle with death, to the death. "One side will have to go," Larkin wrote in "Aubade." But would it?

It might have been the walks with Ellen while death walked beside us. But I was coming to the idea, or the idea had finally found its way to me, that death had been on the journey all along. The wolf asked whether there were better ways to think of mortality, to see death as an ally of sorts rather than something to be denied and avoided. The closer I got to seventy, the more companionable death felt. What choice did I have? The rude intruder had moved in and he wasn't going home.

There was a lot to be said for optimism. It let you think a thing and then do the thing without doubt or fear slowing you down, and I was grateful for the forward momentum that my inherited condition had given me throughout my life, and happy to see it passed on to Sam. It did tend to blot out the starker reality, though, the hard parts that made the optimism less hollow. I wanted to keep Ellen in the optimistic version of the wolf story. But that meant Ellen couldn't talk to me about death the way she wanted to, now that we were both finally ready.

Tim the Jungian told me about a wolf dream he'd heard years earlier: "The dreamer was watching a young woman walk through a beautiful meadow on a perfect day. Then out of nowhere, a wolf came and tore the woman to pieces."

"Jesus," I said.

"That's what the dreamer said." Tim gave me a look. "The wolf challenges our naive and one-sided need for a positive outlook. It's the innocent blindness to the dark side that needs to be killed."

The story of Nick and the wolf changed every time it got told. Likely it'll change again. There's no need to see the life-and-death struggle one way or the other. Old friend or no friend; the hut or the highway; divorced or still, fundamentally, married. Even when we're alone all the versions of our stories keep us company. Neither side has to go.

Except when someone dies, they do have to go.

"I understand that 'wherever' isn't necessarily here with us," Sam had said about where Nick was going.

Ellen here. Ellen no longer here. The space between those two things is untraversable.

sixteen

NEW LOVE

WHEN HE WALKS INTO A room, you know he's there. It's not his perfectly proportioned stature, though that's easy to linger on. It's not his devastating good looks: straight brown hair with the kind of highlights you pay money for— golden, to match his smooth, unlined skin. It's not even the watch-what-I-do-next grin slapped on his face, although whatever he does next will for sure take you by surprise—he's that kind of original, unfettered thinker.

Dressed in blue pinstriped shorts to the knee, a loose-fitting orange T-shirt, ankle socks, and black runners, he's the type it's tempting to describe as unconcerned about his appearance. But that's not quite right, because he's been known to enumerate every item of his clothing to a willing listener. It's more that he's confident in his audience. His laid-back style isn't trying to win anyone over; he's already won.

But what you really notice when he comes into a room is that he walks up to you, arms hanging loose at his sides, deceptively relaxed, and shouts: "*YAAAAAAAAAAAAAAAA-YAAAAAAAAAAAAAAA!*"

I, Yaya, open my arms, but he's already running for the kitchen, where he finds what he seeks: the silver key to the hut that is mine alone. "I want it, Yaya. I really, really want it."

Understanding what my grandson, at two years and two months, wants from me, at sixty-eight, could be the key—why not call it that?—to understanding the grandbaby-grandparent relationship in the middle years of the 2020s. People talk about the "grandparent redo," fixing all the things you did wrong with your own kids. But that leaves out the wants and hopes of the other person in the relationship. My grandson is the cup with the water pouring in. I'm the cup with the water pouring out. We catch what we can from each other, even as it runs through our fingers as fast as time.

My grandson was born with a head of dark hair—it dwindled to a stripe down the middle of his otherwise bald head for his first year of his life—after a natural labor at a birthing center in the east end of Toronto. He gave a small smile as he lay on his mother's chest. An hour later, he slept in his wicker bassinet on my kitchen table while Ivonne slept upstairs. Three months after that, he'd perfect the trademark smile that would capsize my heart into a lake of love, and I'll apologize here: it's impossible to write about a grandchild with sober detachment. Let's resort to facts for a while.

The new baby was the first grandchild born to either side of his family. This put him at a demographic crossroads, although he didn't know that yet. In 1986, *Newsweek* magazine ran a cover story that set off a panic for many unpartnered women of my generation. "Too Late for Prince Charming?" claimed that college-educated women over forty had a less than 3 percent chance of ever getting married. Today's headline, just as chilling for some of that same generation of women, might be "Too Many Nanas?" Canada is at peak grandparent capacity. There are a record 7.5 million Canadians of grandparenting age, up from 5.4 million in 1995. At the same time, far fewer babies are being born. Potential grandparents outnumber children under the age of fourteen by two million.

We don't need to look beyond our own families to see how we got here. My two sets of grandparents had thirty-three grandchildren between them. My grandparents did not vie for our attention, or at least not by the time I was born. I barely noticed them either, in the rough and tumble of siblings and cousins.

My parents' contribution to the brood was five boomer babies born between 1947 and 1962. Our parents shaped their lives around their children, but they were the rulers, the children the peons, and you'd do well not to forget it. That they seemed indomitable made it easier for the boomers to reject them and everything they stood for, in the mass rite of passage of the 1960s and 1970s. "You've thrown us all aside and put us on our way," The Band sang of their own parents' lament in "Tears of Rage."

My siblings and I went on to produce nine children between us. My parents adored their grandchildren and had meaningful relationships with each of them, often having them to stay. But they also lived their own lives, as they always had. Our nine children have so far produced this one grandchild, all alone at the bottom of the inverted pyramid. "I'm disappointed, but I've accepted it," said my brother David, whose only child decided not to have kids. "I believe it would have been regenerative."

Ivonne postponed returning to her career as a dentist to work full time raising her son. Kelly flourished in a burgeoning medical-tech company and worked mostly from home. On the days he did go into the office, his little family often met him for lunch at a downtown park, where many families seemed to be doing the same. My parents believed that this kind of parental devotion would produce a nasty spoiled child and later a feckless bitter adult who drove an ice cream truck just fast enough that the kids had to run to catch up. But the evidence seems to be to the contrary. It turns out that being loved and cherished and seen and heard in a family with visibly expressed emotions makes for great human beings.

I was one of many. My grandson is one of one, so far. What will this less crowded landscape produce? A ground-shifting social movement seems unlikely, but something more singular, perhaps, will blossom from the heavily fertilized new life. The year he was born, spring was marked not only by the baby's arrival but also, one month later in May, by the arrival of Elisabeth the gardener. She and her crew dug deep into the backyard soil, finding buried rocks and slate as they did. "We'll use them to make a curving path to the hut door"—Elisabeth waved north, away from the hut—"because the eye doesn't want a straight line in a path." The garden she planted beside the path changed with the seasons, and we did too. Ivonne often wore a Marian blue dressing gown with bright pink garden crocs, and Madonna and child stood at the end of the stone path as the blossoms began their first year alongside the baby's.

"Everything that we needed to make this garden was right here under the soil," Elisabeth said on a spring day two years later. (A gardener is a futurist, said Deborah Levy, with a vision of how a plant will grow and blaze in bloom.) Elisabeth had come to survey the progress of the now teen-aged hornbeams, the river birch that was hogging too much space in the narrow yard, and the constellation dogwood that refused to bloom. "It's like all the ingredients were here all along, waiting to be found and made into this garden."

—

"When we study long-term *changes* in consciousness," Owen Barfield wrote in his *History in English Words*, "we are studying changes in the world itself." Barfield was one of the Oxford Inklings of the 1920s, a small group of Christian fantasists that included Tolkien and C.S. Lewis. "Consciousness is not a tiny bit of the world stuck on the rest of it. It is the inside of the whole world." For Barfield, the mind *was* reality, and I loved that. Except that watching my grandson grow, and perhaps being less donnish than the Inklings, I often witnessed how the working of the mind was indivisible from the movement of the body.

"You see here she's going straight, but when she realizes that she's walking toward the couch, she takes a left turn just before she gets there." Ron, Gillian's husband, was showing me a video of his granddaughter's first steps. We were on the third viewing. "Start it again," I said. It was better than a Truffaut movie. "She's thinking ahead, you see," Ron said as I studied her small and serious face. "It's all very smooth and thought out."

These are the kinds of conversations that grandparents find riveting. My friend Matt, in New York, said that formerly interesting friends become as dull as a long lineup upon becoming grandparents. Which was odd, because every grandparent *I* knew had suddenly become utterly compelling. "And the guest rooms that used to be mine when I came to visit have all been turned into rooms for the grandbabies."

I didn't tell him that my own guest room, where Matt had stayed, was now decked out with a crib and colorful prints of lions and giraffes on the walls. Nor did I send him the iPhone video of my grandson's first steps, which like Ron I'd watched maybe thirty times, studying the way mind and body worked together to accomplish this milestone. It was not unlike watching my mother at the other end of life, except the reverse: how her physical timidity began to close off her mind.

A formative experience for my grandson was riding the subway. By the time he was two months old, his mother had learned to navigate the transit system from one end of Toronto to the other: which stops had elevators for the stroller, where to transfer and where not to. The way mothers need to prowl with their babies, to get out. I sometimes joined them. The baby's eyes became huge at the noise and momentum of the trains as they barreled into the stations. Perhaps it was his own motor helplessness, when he couldn't even control his tiny arms, that made him more susceptible to the massive machines that were all motor and movement. Eventually, everything became a subway. A row of blocks, a set of spoons, my lower kitchen cupboards, which were gray like the subway cars. The baby entered and exited the cupboard doors, his imitation of the subway sounds precisely pitched. "Ping, ping, ping: Dupont Station." I was incapable of replicating the sounds to his satisfaction when invited to board the train. "No, Yaya. *Ping ping ping.*" "That's what I just said!" ("The fascinating thing, Mom," said Kelly, "was you arguing with the baby for ten minutes about the accuracy of your *ping ping ping.*" Add loss of pitch to the "have not" list.)

The subway game went deeper than any other with him. When he suddenly lost his own motor ability, I believe his imagination struggled as much as his body. Out of that struggle came the first story he ever told, one with a true dramatic arc.

He'd been playing in the sandbox in the local playground up the street, while his father sat watching on the bench nearby. Nothing had happened in the sandbox, except that after a while, the baby left it and came over and sat in Kelly's lap, and for the next six days he couldn't walk. If he tried to stand up, his leg would collapse out from under him.

Blood tests, ultrasounds, and X-rays were done in the emergency department at Sick Children's Hospital that same day. Hours later, the frightened and exhausted parents went home with no answers and a baby who was still unable to walk. They were told to come back in forty-eight hours if nothing had changed.

"'I don't know' is one of the best things a doctor can say," said D. I'd called him in a dark spiral. "Because 98 percent of the time, you don't know." What you don't want, he said, is a doctor who orders more and more terrifying tests, chasing the most unlikely possibility. "That doesn't serve anyone, the baby least of all."

"I am hurting, Yaya. And I am scared," the baby said when the family came over the next afternoon, words he would repeat over the next few days. "Would you like a Band-Aid?" I said, and we chose one with a picture of Peppa Pig to put over his knee, and over our frightened hearts. He was thoughtful, pensive even. And of course, unusually immobile. I relayed the wait-and-see advice from D to Kelly and Ivonne, because what else could we do?

My grandson's character was revealed in the next week, or perhaps simply the character of being a young human. His essential sweetness, his innocent good cheer, his ability to accept and give love. The trademark smile was not gone, but something new had joined it. You saw it in his eyes as he looked silently out the kitchen window. I tried to follow his calm, and to show my own to his parents. "Your kids are telling you their baby is sick and you're thinking, 'Oh, my God, oh, my God,'" said Meryl, grandmother of six. "But outside you say, 'I'm sure everything is okay.'"

"I'm sure everything's okay," I said to Kelly and Ivonne.

Nothing changed in forty-eight hours. This time I joined the baby and his parents at the hospital. It was a stinking hot summer night in the barely air-conditioned orthopedic wing, where he'd been sent for specialist assessment. The same tests were repeated. Between the long waits for results, we took turns carrying the baby up and down the hallways.

At the nadir of the endless night, two nurses arrived to take blood and attach an intravenous to his arm. This took time and effortful work. Ivonne lay on the cot and tried to breastfeed the bawling baby. I held her head because there was no pillow. Kelly held his arms around his wife and child. We were a tableau of sorrow.

When the nurses left, we dimmed the lights and tried to restore calm. The baby lay beside his mother in hiccups of cries between breastfeeding, eyes wide. And then he sat straight up, put his finger to his forehead—like the Scarecrow reciting complicated math in *The Wizard of Oz* after he learns that he's always had a brain—and told a story.

"Dada took me to a big room. A train was in the ceiling! I heard"—he paused to hold his finger to his ear; this was the first time he'd said the word "heard"—"a loud sound. It was scary. Dada, show Yaya."

My son, grandson, and I set out for this magical room, which was a café in the hospital where Kelly had taken the baby earlier. The boy pointed to the children's train under glass in the ceiling. He showed me where the loud sound had come from—a large freezer that was now quiet. We found unicorns painted on a corner wall, something new to add to the story. And he discovered, and us with him, where stories come from, the well of fears and hopes that make us human. The café story, with its unexpected train and frightening sound, was perhaps a way to describe what he had been through in the hospital, but also to give it some distance.

When we finally left that night with the same instructions—wait forty-eight more hours—Kelly was very frustrated. "We're no further ahead." Except we were. Things hadn't gotten worse, and that was good, the doctor told us; it ruled out a lot of dire and urgent possibilities. It was a real event, not a psychological one, she also said; she could see it in his movements. And she'd allayed our worst fears one by one. As we packed up to leave, tidying up the mess people manage to make even when trapped in a small room for hours, we were all wet with nerves and fatigue. The baby's golden-streaked hair was plastered to his face, and his eyes were bright.

We walked down the long hospital corridor, and he began the second story of his life, summoning up everything that had occurred that night: "Two doctors"—he held up two fingers—"in blue coats. Both scary." He put his finger on his forehead again, and I remembered the first time he'd stuck his index finger in the air to catch a complex thought, pre-language, or perhaps to form such a thought, his eyes following his finger as it attempted to touch the ineffable. But some stories are too dark to tell, and the one of the blue-coated doctors ended at "Both scary," before he leaned back in his stroller, exhausted. Two days later, the baby took his first crablike step. Two days after that, he walked again.

Nancy told me later that the same thing had happened to her son Conor when he was the same age, and they'd never found out what it was. We never did either. But Conor is now a strapping man with a booming voice and a wickedly funny way with a story.

The baby and I walked down the garden path. It was a great relief to see him mobile again. He held the silver key that was his as much as mine and we talked foliage. "These are the native grasses we planted last year," I said. "Look how well they're doing."

He did a sweep with his hand. "Many green grasses." The word "many" was being trotted out a lot: many loud birds, many black cars, look at the many people. To witness his steady change from one word to three to sentences to stories with dramatic arcs was not unlike me writing this book, bringing it into being sentence by sentence. The baby made sure he had my full attention before he lifted his foot and stomped on one of the many green grasses. It was impossible not to laugh.

"You're only going to encourage him," Kelly said from a garden chair.

I pulled myself together. "These are baby grasses. They're only one year old. That's one year younger than you." Very rarely did I offer a lesson. I didn't love the tone of my voice when I did, as if I knew better, which neither of us bought.

We caught what we could from each other, in those proverbial cups. We didn't live in the land of life lessons. The future was the parents' job. My own future was too short and the baby's too endless for us to locate ourselves there. My grandson looked at his father and then at me, his co-conspirator in the lawless present. I shrugged and smiled.

"Many *baby* green grasses!" he said, stomping again.

At dinnertime, the exhaustion of the past week caught up with him. Now he couldn't decide if he wanted a strawberry or a peach.

"No, a peach! No, a strawberry!" He flung himself on his stomach on the floor and sobbed.

"I'm hurting and I'm scared." He peeked up to see how that was landing. He'd faced sorrow, pain, and fear, which was a lot at two years and two months. "Maybe you need a Yaya Band-Aid," his father said calmly as he put the rice and broccoli he'd just roasted onto a bright yellow plate for his son. I won't be able—or even there—to fix every pain and sorrow in his life so simply, but for now. "Blue or pink?" I said.

"Hello, my young friend." We'd walked up to the neighborhood park after dinner, and the man speaking was old. He had an unaggressive, head-down smile and a little dog at his feet. He and my grandson were park acquaintances. "How old are you now?"

"Two years old." The baby held two fingers up, for clarity. Finger-counting was a habit we shared. Along with how many hours I'd slept, among other domestic tallies, I had begun to count how many years the baby and I had left in each other's lives. When I was seventy-eight, he would be—I counted on my fingers—twelve. If I lived to ninety, he'd be . . . twenty-four. I could see him graduate from university, maybe fall in love.

"Two is a good age," the old man said. "It's all over at four." I'd read this too, that the human brain has its most unfettered growth in the first four years, and the man and I chatted about this until the baby noticed a woman slowly approaching. If the man I was chatting with was old, this woman was very, very old. She had long white hair and paused between each step as she bent low over her walker. I put her at maybe ninety-two and resisted the urge to count on my fingers how many years I had until then (twenty-four). I was young yet. Aunt Helen had been right about that.

"Look! Other yaya," my grandson said to me. And in case I didn't get his drift, he pointed to me—"my yaya"—and then back to the very, very old woman—"other yaya." I considered arguing with a two-year-old, but I knew I'd lose. He'd proven his skills as a narrator, both succinct and honest. The man shrugged his shoulders and gave me his downward smile. "You're more stylish," he said, and then he walked on with his little dog trotting at his feet.

seventeen

INTERLUDE

I DIDN'T KNOW WHEN I started this book that I was going to buy a map.

I didn't know that as I sat in my hut on a blank February morning (blank sky, blank page), an old friend would write to me, and then become a new person in my life, and a character in my story.

I *did* know the travel iron would make it in. In fact, I considered calling this book *Travel Irons and Other Stories*. I knew, too, that I was on a trip to old, wherever that would take me.

I didn't know that bringing real people into the story would alter my relationships with them out in the world. This was a failure of imagination; I see that now.

I didn't know I had finished this book, either, until here I am, a few chapters from the end, close enough to see the edge of the map just ahead.

"Books are your fate," said Hisham Matar in an interview about his novel, *My Friends*. In the time that you write a book, you are also being written by it. His terrific interviewer, Alex Clarke, who talked to him on a stage in Paris (you can watch it on YouTube), had the good sense to stay with this tangent. "If the book is in some sense—and you may be talking on a metaphorical level or you may not—your fate," she said, "can you change your fate in the writing of it?"

Matar leaned back in his chair to consider her question. He was a thoughtful writer and stirring to listen to. "In some ways, the companionship of the book you are writing is an emotional and intellectual companionship," he said, "and like all of the other relationships we have in our life, we are cultivated by them, and they educate us."

Near the end of this story, and the end of my own decade, I'd like to pause and share share my recent education as I wrote this book, and it wrote me.

This is a work of non-fiction. I've often longed for what I imagined was the freedom of "autofiction," as it's fashionably called—the autobiographical novel, nonfiction novel, *roman à clef,* choose your nomenclature. (Sheila Heti delightfully jettisoned the whole debate during a Toronto staged interview about her brilliantly frank and seeking *Alphabetical Diaries,* which has been variously described by her international publishers as essays, a novel, and a memoir: "Why can't we just call it a book?" she said.) But my brain goes *zzzzzzt* whenever I try to understand what autofiction is. I stubbornly—timidly?— cleave to facts, even as my relationship with them has evolved.

Early in my career as a journalist, there was a brutal allegiance to getting at the truth. Reporters often "doorstopped" their subjects, literally putting their foot in the door to force their way into someone's office or home, sometimes with cameras running behind them. I occasionally miss the certitude of that mentality, but not its righteous monomania. Part of the answer to "where are we now" is always "together." Living with the people inside the book who are also outside the book can feel crowded. It's perhaps not conducive to the freedom writing wants. But my story is their story too, so I've shared what I wrote of them, with them.

Some offered a better way of landing a line they'd said (and thank you). Sometimes people corrected a simple fact. "Not that it matters," Ron said, but in the video of his granddaughter taking her first steps, she turned left and not right as I had written. He re-sent me the video to verify it—and my God, I loved that, because nailing a factual detail brings the truth home in the easiest way possible. Sometimes there were requests for consequential changes. Other times, the asks were so alluringly inconsequential they gave a new insight into the person that I immediately wanted to add to the story. (That's the take-no-prisoners side of journalism any subject rightly fears.)

"It's not D, it's your story of D, for you to write as you choose," said D as he urged me to finish the book. And then became scarce while I did. No one wants to feel like they're "material," and ultimately almost everything is. It's a risk to put someone on the page. For me, that risk has been whether writing about other people will scatter them or keep them close.

"As soon as you write it down, you begin to lie," Ellen said. Writers can go two ways when being written about themselves. One is to be supremely unruffled, as she was, because the person on the page is not them. The other is to mistrust any narrator but themselves, because the person on the page is them.

"You're writing your version of your friend named Ellen," said Ellen.

"Wait." I help up my hand. "Let me get a pen to write this down."

I spent the next five minutes rummaging around the kitchen drawers at Tim and Nancy's cottage, where Ellen and I had come to spend a quiet week in the disconcertingly warm days of November. The cottage was near the tiny northern Ontario hamlet of Magnetawan, where we bought T-shirts at the local hardware store with the words DOWNTOWN MAGNETAWAN emblazoned across the front. Once a day we'd walk Sally along the gravel road rimmed with tall and leafless birch trees, their white bark shooting light in the sun. "Run in the woods, Sally!" said Ellen, but of course Sally did not.

"I need to start thinking about Sally," Ellen said.

"Not yet, though," I said.

"Soon, though," she said.

Outside of those brief excursions, Ellen and I were two dormant creatures, each sleeping for twelve hours a day— Ellen in her illness, me in an end-of-book stupor, as well as a fog of grief about my friend, although I hardly knew it. An hour or so after waking up from a ten-hour sleep, we'd shuffle back to our rooms (Ellen had the master bedroom with the picture of the wolf on the wall) for a morning nap, soon to be followed by a second nap in the afternoon. At night we built tall, cracking fires in the huge stone fireplace and watched *Downton Abbey* on my computer. The blackness outside pressed against the broad windows, erasing our view of the stern winter lake. Sally, who slept behind us on the couch, would sometimes leap to her feet to bark at things we could not see, waking us up from nap number three, the pre-bed snooze. You can discover new things about a person, even after you've known them for forty years, if you spend a week in their steady company on a quiet northern lake with no internet. Such as, at the same time I was starting out at *Gifts and Tablewares* magazine, Ellen was an editor at *Plateworld: The Magazine of Fine Art and China*.

"I had no idea!" I couldn't believe the coincidence.

"Yes you did. I told you. You just weren't listening. They flew me to Chicago for a 'plateworld' fair." She said this smugly, I felt. "I sometimes wonder why I ever left that magazine." She paused. "Or maybe it was Cleveland."

"There's a big difference between Cleveland and Chicago," I sniffed. Professional rivalry never ends.

"Continue about the lying," I said, the fire hot on my face; I'd found a pen.

"My own version is different from yours," said Ellen. "But that doesn't make yours not valid or untrue."

"Except the written version tends to supplant reality, once you put it on the page," I said. I've noticed how after I write it down, my version becomes the only way the people tell the story after that. Just as I'm being changed by this book, so are the people in it with me. It's solipsistic, but not incorrect. Ellen and I didn't really talk about how sick she was until I wrote that in my book, and then we could. And did again, as we sat side-by-side looking into the fire. "I asked D how it would be at the end." Ellen continued to speak to her own doctor D every week; he helped her decipher the incomprehensible medical reports. "Hopefully I'll just get sleepier and sleepier, he told me. Which doesn't sound too bad." She leaned forward and turned on the next episode of *Downton*. Fifteen minutes later, we'd both drifted off, two old friends in their easy chairs in front of the dimming fire.

I asked Ann how she felt about being a character in the book on a recent sibling trip to Tofino, British Columbia, where we two youngest shared a king-sized bed. We often chatted in the mornings, our faces very near to each other on our pillows. Ann looked pretty in the day's first light, her face fresh from sleep and her dark hair across the pillow.

"You moan in your sleep, Cathrin," she said one morning.

"Moan, like how?"

Ann answered my question with a long moan that sounded like a very old ghost trying to heave herself out of her grave. We laughed until the bed shook.

"It's like a photographer snapping you," Ann eventually answered. "And you think, *Wait, that's not what I look like.* Or not the only way I look," she said. "But I have the willingness and trust to let go of my version so the book can land the way it wants." Ann poked me in the arm to drive home her point, then held her hand in the air, caught mid-act. "Ha!" She poked me again. "You see? You get to decide what to keep in or take out. But those decisions are constantly being informed by your biases about all of us in the book, which affects your assessment of what to include."

Ann is a poker. Ann does not see herself as a poker. But her poking, and my demented reactions to her poking throughout this book, are a shortcut to a truth about the bracing familiarity, murderous irritation, and unstoppable love you have for a sibling with whom you've shared beds, rooms, and houses, on and off, through most of your life. I suppose if Ann were writing this book, I'd be a moaner. Which I don't love. But I'm writing it, so Ann's a poker.

Sometimes a scene or moment I described had meaning for someone that was bigger than what I put on the page. The facts weren't wrong, but the emotion was. This is where the novelist has the upper hand. When you're inside Isabel Archer's mind through her devastating marriage in *Portrait of a Lady*, it's Henry James's secret access that lets you travel miles into her character, until he reels you back into the action with a new line of dialogue. The distance is shorter in non-fiction, when a person's interior is expressed by what they say and do rather than by what they think and feel. Sam's story of his cousin and the wolf on the road was emotionally charged, I could see that listening to him, but I didn't presume to write what he was feeling. Until he called later to describe that for me. Did that make it more true? I'm not sure. Like I said, I used to be more certain about truth than I am now.

My daughter Mary, who at thirty can still actually recall conversations verbatim, told me she "remembered saying those things exactly as you wrote them. But my character is so confident and certain, way more than the real Mary. You write me with a lot more conviction than I feel." The older we get, the more indomitable our children seem. Of course, I also know my daughter's vulnerabilities and worries, but I was interested to hear that they had not come out on the page, or not for her. Does that make it not Mary?

A book, this book, in a strange way, doesn't really care about anyone in it, not me or anyone else. But I do. That kind of caring isn't separate from a respect for writing itself, which in many ways is an act of consideration toward your readers: keeping them apace, not confusing or tricking or boring them, being conscious of your responsibility as their guide, with as little arrogance as possible. Good writing is often good manners, somebody once said. Another way writing cultivates us.

Writing's full of surprises, too. It pulls reality into itself. I knew I'd write about the discovery of that secret passageway to my mother. Who could resist? But not that a two-year-old would show me the real secret of the passageway, just as I was about to finish the book.

eighteen

A TALLY, PART 3: HAVE

FORGET THE "HAVE NOT" NOW. We forge ahead.

Have:

1. The time ahead of me, but not too much. On the final night at the cottage with Ellen, I opened my eyes in bed—as with my sudden thought of the map, it was once again three a.m., a universally popular hour to startle from sleep; the hour for witches, angels, peeing and epiphanies, depending on your proclivities—and saw my place in time. Visually, I mean. I pictured a string as far as I could reach between my outstretched arms. Go ahead, stretch out your arms and look at your own imaginary string. That's your life. Your string of life. For as long as you can remember, you've been on the first inch of that string. Sure, when you get somewhere into your fifties, that most uninteresting of decades, you have an inkling you can't stay in that first inch forever. But you don't really believe it, because there's still plenty of string ahead. What happens next—so fast you missed it—is you're all the

way at the far end of the string, shoved along like a bead on an abacus, *click-clack*, and instead of an inch behind you, there's only an inch left ahead of you. Your long past has now become a short future. But I still have my inch. I'll take it.

2. The past behind me. It's noisier than it used to be. Early on in this book, I chose a tally to understand where I was, because I didn't want the judgement that a reckoning insists on. But lately my past has its own ideas about how to present itself. It's become a tribunal. Mostly at night, my life unspools in my mind like a movie I watch with a combination of ambivalence, dread, and longing. Much of it is grievously inconsequential, the smallest slight given or received, a comfort withheld, a stinginess of my own spirit that comes back to torment me like a stone in my shoe. But there are three big themes.

There's my career. The jobs I wish I'd been spared, and the men I wish I hadn't answered to. So much striving. And failing. And striving again. I relive those jobs in my sleep, worse, better, differently.

My children, and the things I'd change if I could live my life with them over again. Actually, it would be great to just live my life with them over again, even if I did everything exactly the same the second time around. I did my best with the information available to me at the time, is what I tell them, and myself.

Down comes the gavel again: let's not pass over the epic fails with the men I have loved. My tribunal certainly doesn't. It notes my inability not only to clearly see who I was in love with, but to see who *I* was as a woman in love, and then to say it out loud: this is me, this is what I long for, this is what I hope we can yet be.

Stop judging, I say to my nightly tribunal, but it isn't listening. So far.

3. My beloved writers. I've gone all-in with writers and the characters they create since *The Tales of Peter Rabbit*. It was the first story I read on my own and then I scoured my small world for everything I could find about that well-dressed, carrot-crazed rabbit. I did the same as a teenager with the writers who carried me away, marauding the Grimsby Public Library like a pirate looking for gold. The pantheon of authors we carry in our heads may not know they're there, but they're as present and alive as our friends, and as lasting.

I've introduced some of them in this book, and I thank them for being here.

4. The dark side. Come on in. (But don't stay long.) I had no plan to watch the total eclipse of 2024. It was cloudy in Toronto that day, my neighbourhood is flat, and there are a lot of trees blocking the view of the sky above. Plus, it was

a busy afternoon at home, me writing in the hut, Mary working in the garden. But then, without using any words, Mary and I decided in unison to set out up the street to see what we could see.

Sibelius Park was full when we got there. The mood was a little bit spooky but also a little bit lively as it began to get dark. Not pitch black. "More like a very dim room," said Mary. The streetlights popped on and there was a feeling of uncertainty about what might happen next.

"Look how the darkness rises," I said quietly to Mary, pointing at our feet. "Instead of coming down the way it does at night, it's rising up from the ground."

"*The Dark Knight Rises*," said Mary. And then, a moment later, "That's it."

"What do you mean, that's it?"

"The eclipse is over. It's already getting brighter." It was true, although the streetlights remained lit in the middle of the afternoon as we left the park.

"Look, our house light has come on," I said. It was a homey feeling to see the lantern shining above the blue door, like a light at the top of the stairs at night, guiding you: this way up. The darkness came from below like a sigh from the earth. The daylight overhead met it halfway. It was only a moment in time, but I saw them together, the light and the dark, and it felt companiable.

5. I am divorced. I've accepted my divorce, finally, as a new way to be. I got to the end of the long tail. I'm excited to see where it will flick me.

6. The trees. Look up.

7. An unexpected happiness. With my sixties mostly behind me, I think it may have been my happiest decade. I don't know if happiness at sixty-eight is a decision or that inherited condition again, or perhaps a biological switch toward late-life joy; likely all three. Martin Amis, a self-proclaimed optimist, called it your destined mood. "At a certain point, usually in late middle age, something congeals and solidifies and encysts itself—and that's your lot, that's your destiny." Amis was about my age when he wrote *Inside Story*. I finally understood autofiction as I read that book, and then it slipped away from me the moment I was done—like hearing someone brilliantly explain string theory and *totally getting it*, until they stopped talking. "You're going to feel this way for the rest of your life," Amis continued. "You have found your des-tined mood, and it has found you, too."

James Hillman, author and Jungian, described it as "the force of character," in his book by the same name. Old age is not about beating death, as in a contest, he said, but rather about finally finding our vitality and character, which age makes stronger.

"You can become bigger or bitter, this is what I think," wrote Elizabeth Strout toward the end of *Lucy by the Sea*. Doubling down on the most inflexible version of yourself—in my case impatient, quickly bored, and with an overdeveloped sense of aggrievement—is alluring, especially when confronted with loss, illness, betrayal, or disappointment. No one gets out alive. We end. It can be hard to imagine the world going on without us in it. It will though. But (here comes the optimism again) what if we don't need to fear old age, but rather welcome it as an arrival? Of who our best self might yet be, the one that people will remember us as? Speaking of which . . .

8. My grandson showed me the real meaning of the passageway not long ago.

"Follow me," I said to him as we put on our matching pink Crocs and walked to the back of my garden. Kelly and his family had found a bigger, better apartment than the one they first moved into when they left my place—and in a stroke of luck, it was on the next street over, in a house whose lot backed directly onto my own. I quickly hatched a plan to put in a child-sized gate for my grandson to pass from his backyard into mine. His own secret portal from one place to the other. I lay awake at night with excitement at the thought. Kelly and Ivonne were in on the idea, though not as gripped by it as me.

Neither was the baby, it turned out. "You pull this string"—I showed him the gate, hidden by the hornbeam trees. "And then"—the gate opened. "Look, there's your house, on the other side." "How about a snack, Yaya," he said. But a couple of hours later, the gate took hold of his imagination, and likely will never let go, not entirely.

"There is a gate. In the backyard," he said slowly, not to me but to the space between us. In the days and weeks that followed, he would stand in the open gateway, going neither in nor out, saying, "My house. Yaya's house." This could go for forty minutes, the little boy in the portal. This is where we are, he showed me. On the verge. Not here or there, but in the doorway between.

9. New wheels. But that's another story . . . one more story, coming up.

nineteen

ON THE ROAD, PART 3: WILD AND SAVAGE

"STEP RIGHT UP!" A MAN in an orange vest opened the barrier to Gate 12, making me the first in line for my Megabus from Toronto to St. Catharines. When other travelers asked the orange-vested man for directions to their own buses, he was rude: "You're never going to make that bus, and good luck to you!" Except he clearly had no well-wishes for anyone who was not a Megabus traveler. I was sorry for the people who wouldn't catch their buses, but inwardly thrilled at my own choice, bus-wise.

"Where's the Megabus?" I asked the orange-vested man when the doors to Gate 12 opened to a regular-sized bus. I'd been imagining riding on a double-decker. Maybe not on top of the world, but on top of the bus.

"Megabus is the name of the company," he said. "The buses come in all sizes."

I quelled my disappointment at not being part of the mega-universe and took a seat at the front. The day I rode the GO Train to the map library, at the beginning of my quest to understand where I was headed, my view was backward. Now, going to the city where I began, I'd look ahead—there are no rear-facing seats on a bus, but it was also by inclination. The distance was again short, just a couple of hours down the road. I almost want to apologize for taking you only two inches on the map, to the other side of the lake, in the end. But it would turn out to be one of the best trips I've had in many years. It made me think about why we go anywhere, and the value of what we find when we do.

The bus pulled out of the station, and my phone flashed.

Ookpik is riveted by Love Is Blind UK. My friend Tecca, the one with the tidy crawlspace, texted a picture of her new Ookpik, a four-inch-tall sealskin snowy owl with huge eyes, watching TV beside her. As the bus passed through Hamilton, Fruitland, and Grimsby, Tecca and I engaged in a complex series of overlapping messages about recipes for a weekend away, a sheet sale at an uptown bedding store, dinner with Ellen, real estate (because already the conversation had begun about when we should sell our houses), and the Ookpik I had just given her for her seventieth birthday. Ookpiks were to the 1960s what travel irons were to the 1970s, so when Maria, my border, came home from Iqaluit with an assortment of Ookpiks made by Inuit elders, I bought one with wings to give to Tecca.

"Are you kidding me?" she said when she opened it. "This was my favorite thing at seven, and now at seventy he's come back into my life."

"The wings are to help you fly to whatever is next," I'd said, because she'd just retired, and I knew how that could make you want to sit tight.

I too am hooked on Love Is Blind UK, I typed. *I love their accents. Be right back, I have to pee.*

The toilet at the back of the bus was not mega. It was the size of a matchstick. There was no sink, for example, and no light that I could locate. I pushed the only visible button I could find, to flush. As I slowly swayed back toward my seat—bus drivers go like there's no tomorrow, and there might not be, the way they careen across lanes—the intercom scratched on. "Please do not push the emergency alarm in the bathroom unless you have an emergency." All heads swung to look at me.

Mega-centered out! I texted Tecca.

Mega-pee! she texted back.

My brother David was sitting on a bench at the St. Catharines bus terminal as mine pulled in. He was wearing a blue T-shirt with a drawing of a wolf.

"Is that Sam's wolf?" I asked.

"It is not," he said. "I got it at Giant Tiger for ten dollars."

In the car David took the passenger seat, as he does, me the back seat, as I do. "What's the plan, Tim?" I said.

"Let's go plan-free," said Tim. I had a loose idea of the day—to see the house where I'd been born, the plot where our parents were buried, and other places we'd located in St. Catharines at the birthday party when I'd spread my map over the dining-room table, excited for everyone to see.

"Where's that bridge over the wide expanse?" I wanted to know as Tim drove through the main drag of town.

"That's the highway now," Tim said. The city had been intersected by an expressway in the 1980s. My father was pleased how fast it made getting in and out of town. *But what town?* I thought now. The bland flattening of towns and cities by superhighways and superstores into non-places that could be anywhere—that sadness will stay with me. "It's painful to see," said Tim. And so we set out on our no-plan tour, darkened but not defeated by the road we took.

"How about a coffee to perk us up?" I said. The coffee shop took us near the house where our aunt Mary had lived, and where her husband, our uncle Bill, had died of lung cancer in his sixties; a cancer that is now survivable, thanks to medical volunteers like Ellen. The pretty white wooden house sat on a large, treed lot overlooking the Henley River, where the Royal Canadian Henley Regatta was taking place this very day. I'd stayed in this house when I was in my twenties to help my aunt pack up after her husband died. It was an orderly home, elegantly but sparsely furnished, though much was tucked away, I would discover. They'd never gotten past that Depression-era sense that they might run out, that there wouldn't be enough. The things we hold onto also hold our feelings.

"Come here!" David was excitedly swinging his arm in a wide circle above his head. A woman holding a basket of tomatoes she had just picked from her garden stood beside him with a noncommittal look on her face. "This is Dr. Hunt's daughter-in-law," David introduced us. "She lives here now with Dr. Hunt's son." Earl Hunt had been our family doctor, and our aunt Mary had worked for him most of her life. He delivered me at the Hotel Dieu Hospital in St. Catharines, so I suppose he was the first human being to touch me. He reported news of my arrival on an index card that my mother kept until she died, and that I now keep: "Rashy and excitable." An assessment that remains true.

Pretty soon Dr. Hunt's son joined us and we talked for some time about our aunt and his father, who was revered by our parents and feared by us kids because he didn't believe in anesthetic for things like stitches or pierced ears. "Mary was gleefully indiscreet," I said. "We got to know about everyone's ailments and sex lives." Don't waste the stories that land in your lap—I learned that from her. "All of my siblings are going to be here this afternoon," he said as the eight-person regatta boats slid silently by on the river below. "I can't wait to tell them about this conversation."

"This is the beauty of a no-plan plan," said Tim as we drove away. "You end up in the right place at the right time. One minute later, and she would have been inside with her tomatoes, and we'd have missed her." We all marveled at that, and that will stay with me too: our marveling.

"Hey, do you guys remember Dr. Hunt's white medicine?" I asked from the back seat. "The one in the brown bottle that Mom kept in the door of the fridge?"

"Mom told me Dr. Hunt was taken to court for his homemade medicines, but won the case," said David.

"No kidding?" This was new information, although perhaps not surprising. When I got my own family doctor in Toronto in my twenties, I asked if he had any of that white medicine. I was anxious, and it was a cure-all. "Do me a favor and never take that white medicine again," my new doctor said.

"What do you think was in it?" I asked. David would often take a slug with me as we hung on the open fridge door.

"Some kind of opiate," he said. "Maybe actually opium. Dr. Hunt told Mom, 'Whenever the kids need to calm down, just give them a couple of teaspoons.'"

"That explains more than it might." When my daughter, Mary (named after my dear aunt), had asked if something had happened in my life that made me nervous, I'd said that I was born that way, but the white medicine gave me false hope that the fix was outside myself. Or even that there was a fix. I thought about how we paid careful attention when my grandson told us, "I'm sad and I'm frightened," after he couldn't walk. If I'd said those words as a child it would have gone down in family lore as *hilarious*. "Remember the time she said she was 'sad and frightened'? Har Har!" I don't blame anyone. This was standard-issue parenting at the time. Validation was a long way off. "My mother would've thwacked me on the head with a hairbrush if I'd dared to express an inner fear or worry," said a friend. The feelings we hold onto also hold onto us. That's true too.

"There's Christ the King School," Tim was saying as we drove past our primary school, now boarded up, and Miss Purser with her pointer, my terrifying Grade 1 teacher, popped into my mind and then vanished, I hoped for all time. Next our no-plan tour took us to our wartime bungalow, looking the worse for wear. St. Catharines bungalows haven't changed from when they were built in the booming 1950s, except that they now housed families newly arrived from India and the Philippines. This one was about the same age as we were and (like us now) lopsided, with a red maple tree that seemed to be growing out of the front steps. The lawn's mowed grass was turning brown on top of the struggling green grass underneath. The whole setup looked as eccentric as we did while we posed for a couple of selfies with the house behind us. Our smiles for the camera were rueful. Our days were numbered, the house and us. A disquiet came over me.

"What about the gully?" I asked, thinking of the gully at the end of the street where men had burned campfires, getting closer to my unsettled feeling.

"It's still here," said David. In fact, it ran right behind our house to the end of the street. The gully wasn't "the wild," as we called the north, that glorious land of bent trees and huge rocks the Group of Seven painted. When you went to "the wild" as a kid, you knew you weren't home anymore. The gully was in between wild and domestic. It was one of those uninhabited places that exist at the ends of streets in towns and cities that are still being developed. But its proximity to our domestic life gave it a vivid place in our imagination. "We could stand at our back door and see the campfires burning."

"Who were those men?" I asked for the second time since I'd bought my map of St. Catharines. I think it was their homelessness that made them stay with me. I had always had a roof over my head, starting in this tiny bungalow we stood in front of, and sixty-eight years later in my house with four sides of windows in Toronto. But there too, not far from where I live, are the encampments in the city's parks. The arguments that go on about them are the same as when I was a child. What is home, where is home, who has a home, who does not, and why? "It's hard to say who those men were," said David. "Women too. Mom worried. But Dad would say it was fine, they were just people on the move."

Mom and Dad. My parents, a faintness of them, were with us on the tour, dimmer here, brighter there. Tim drove us to their final home, in the large local cemetery, where none of us had been since we'd buried their urns side by side eight years earlier. The tombstone for our mother's parents we noticed right away. Simple granite, simply adorned with the name Kelly and a single cross. "It's lovely," I said, running my hand along the name. Two footstones with the details of Catherine and James Kelly, my mother's parents, told me they died when I was four, cancelling what I thought were memories of them sitting in our Grimsby living room. They would have been gone for several years by then, so I wondered who that old man was, giving me sticky candy from his pocket.

"Where are Mom and Dad?" I was pacing around, confused. We eventually found a single footstone that seemed to be attached to a completely different grave. "What is it doing over here?" I said. "And why is there only one of them?"

"We made that decision at the time," David said. "We decided on a rose of Sharon bush and one footstone."

"Where is that rose of Sharon?" There were many in bloom all around us, but not here.

"Dead and gone," said David, not one to sugarcoat.

Tim hung his head over the randomly placed single footstone with the name Bradbury carved into it.

"I'm sorry, Mom and Dad," he said. "We knew not."

"Yes, we did," said David. "We all agreed to keep it simple."

"Keep it cheap, more like it," said Tim. Then he had a brain wave. We'd add our parents' name to the lovely Kelly tombstone and center it between the two plots. Horning in on the

thoughtful way our mother and her sisters had commemo-
rated their parents.

"That's our cheap side coming out again, Tim," I said. We
stayed there for a long time, circling the plot and cracking
jokes about how far we'd go to save a few bucks. But it got to
us. I thought about the end of my own road, M-O-R-T, at
my own cemetery plot, and how I'd feel if this crooked footstone was all my kids sprang for.

"Who wants a cemetery plot anyway?" said David.

"I do," Tim said.

"With a proper marker," I added.

"You'll be dead," said David, but I suddenly strongly felt
the need to be visited after I was. "Here I am!" said my
ghost. To have someone run their hand along my name
carved in the tombstone and let me linger in their thoughts
as I shadowed them safely home. When so many people
have no body to mourn, for us to have that certainty about
where our parents were, and to slough it off?

"Get in the car," said Tim. He drove us to the cemetery
office, with that family habit to think a thing and then do it,
no space between the two. The words above the doorbell
said, "By Appointment Only," but we rang anyway. Two
men, one tall and one short, both thickly spectacled, opened
the door and blocked it at the same time. "If you have a problem with your site, you need to email the funeral registry,"
said the short man. But our story of the forlorn footstone

won them over, and five minutes later both men were peering through their glasses at ancient maps and handwritten index cards that proved we owned the two-body plot next to our grandparents and could easily erect a stone there, or at least move that wayward footstone.

"Let's go look," said the tall cemetery man, and we hopped in our cars again. "That's a funny place to put a footer all right," he said. "You see, usually they are lined up with the headstone." Tim bowed his head again, then made the next on-the-spot decision to head for the monument store, very nearby. "Just say BROB sent you," said the tall cemetery man.

Tim and I both stared. "Did you say Bob or Rob?" asked Tim.

"That's a very good question," the man said. "I was born Bob, but when I divorced and dated online, 150 women called me Rob, so I became Rob. My brother's name is Blair, and I used to make fun of it until my mother said, 'Well, your name is BROB, so you're a fine one to talk.'"

Bob-Rob went on for quite a while. "I had a nap in the car," said David afterwards. But his name did hold us in good stead at the monument store. "Isn't Rob wonderful?" the woman said, and I agreed he did have something, in spite of his proximity to death. Or maybe because of it. A bit of graveyard frisson passes for sexy at sixty-eight. They priced us out a smaller granite tombstone that would match the Kelly stone.

"So, we own this whole two-body plot?" said David, the wheels turning.

"That's right," the monument woman said.

"How many urns could we put in there?"

"Eight."

"You think I want to be crowded in with you two for all eternity?" I said as we drove away, although it would quintuple the chance of being visited if all five siblings were popped in there together. And what a steal.

It rained like it was the end of time on the bus ride home. At my feet was a bag of carrots, zucchini, radishes, and lettuces from my brothers' vegetable garden on the Commune. I had more foot room than on the way there; this bus was bigger, but still not mega. We were stuck in traffic for two hours, thanks to the downpour, so I had to pee again, but fortunately the bathroom was larger, with a light, a sink, and a clearly labeled "Flush" button. As I looked into the mirror over the sink, I was surprised that I could see the whole bus and everyone on it behind me—perhaps the door featured some kind of two-way mirror?—until I stood up and realized that the sliding door to the bathroom was open.

Yeesh, I texted Meryl this time. *Who knows how that happened.*

Words like "Who knows" and "I don't know why" and "I'm okay with that"—about more consequential things than an open bathroom door on a bus—were coming out of my mouth a lot. The ease with which this had happened—how I'd become so chill about so much as a woman of nearly seventy; how my ferocious and ceaseless caring about everything all the time had vanished so quickly—made me wonder if I'd had a stroke. There was still the worry about simple things (bathroom door). More all the time. But I'd become almost insanely sanguine about the big stuff. I remembered Aunt Mary saying she worried less about death the closer it got; she'd have been in her late seventies at the time and would die at eighty. Maybe death comes over you, like retiring or moving; a forward-looking new mindset to help get you ready for the final trip.

I sent Meryl the picture of me and my brothers in front of our childhood home first—*a bit to the right and that maple tree would be a nice accent,* she texted back—and then a picture of the single footstone shame-circled in red. I'd been to Meryl's parents' plot, with interlocking wedding rings on a large headstone on top of the Grimsby escarpment, so I should've been embarrassed to show her how little we had done for my own parents, whom she also loved. But shame had joined the slag heap of pointless emotions.

In other news, it's possible D has left although he says he hasn't. D was back to missing me again, even though I was right here. Perhaps it was the place he preferred most, the missing and being missed. "Thinking of you with the change of seasons," he wrote after a considerable silence. "And realizing that time is slipping by. For me, it's about letting myself feel sad."

And how are you about this? Meryl texted back.

He'll return when he's ready. Or he won't.

"Love comes in so many different forms, but it is always love," said Elizabeth Strout's Lucy Barton. "If it is love, then it is love."

"Why I love you is the wrong question," said D.

I never found out what the right question was. Or why love landed where it did. An old friend, a new grandchild, a stranger running down the street with his legs high in the winter cold, the beautiful youth of his stride and the joy I felt—the love—when I stood still to watch him lilt by. Love is not thwarted when it is not noticed or returned or wanted. It's like piling sticks over a rivulet; the water finds a new direction. Love is plucky that way.

I texted *bye* to Meryl and put my phone in my bag. We were by now completely stalled on the wet highway. The rain was orchestral: cymbal crashes on the metal roof; a violin vibrato against the windows. I tried to see which town we were near, but there was no view. It was like being moored in a submarine on the bottom of a very noisy ocean floor. The water moved all around the gray metal tube I was trapped inside, but we did not move. I counted on my fingers how many hours it would be before I could lie in my own bed.

It had been a long day. You could go far, in our over-touristing times, when the planet can hardly bear it. Except that I found that kind of travel more alienating every time I did it. It was this very short jaunt to St. Catharines, in which I had great conversations, solved the mystery of the white medicine, and resolved to mark my parents' last place with more care, where the steady connections made me feel like a traveler again. Going back to St. Catharines gave me the precise and uncomplicated conviction that the world was available to me right where I was. Not as a choice between staying put or setting out, but as a defining truth. It was strange to think that two inches along the map would take me the greatest distance toward understanding the question I asked at the beginning of this book. Where we are now is who we are now.

"What is age but becoming who you are?" I asked earlier in this book. I'm a woman leaving the foothills of her late sixties and beginning to climb the bare ascent. I have a more visceral—*earthier*—idea of where I'm headed after that visit to the cemetery. And I'll be arriving sooner than I'd like. That won't change. Until then, I'll be traveling with the people I love, literary and real, dead and alive. It won't be too far. I guess by now that won't surprise you.

—

"I got an e-bike." I called Ellen to tell her the news. It was adorably French, teal blue, and compact enough to be mistaken for a regular two-wheeler.

"Great. Let me know when you're on it, and I'll be sure to stay inside that day."

"It goes really fast. I wonder how far I'll get?"

"Bloor and Spadina." That was two blocks away.

"I'm going to the lake," I said. I've talked quite a lot about the lake in this book. For nearly seventy years, I've located myself on the west corner of Lake Ontario, that life-shaping body of water, and either ignored or responded to its pull. Lately mostly ignored. My visits were inconstant, though my fealty was not. We were in our own eternal return, the lake and me. This seemed to be true for many people lucky enough to have lived near water, or perhaps traveled to an ocean, river, lake, or bay in their youthful summers and then carried the relationship like a friend they're sure of though rarely see. No matter how far you go you can return to some of your earliest memories when you think of the water they live on. Some people describe their attachment to a particular light over the sea, or the quality of the breeze on a river, or the quicksilver surface and unchanging depth of a big bay. Some feel that swimming alters not just the shape of the water but also, briefly, themselves. Or how they can bask in the sound of the water, like a balm or a blessing. Gillian's mother died in this year, at the age of ninety-four. The last mother to go, of anyone I knew. At the funeral, Gillian spoke about the importance of the town where she grew up, and how her parents had given her the gift of always knowing where she was and so also of always knowing who she was. After the funeral, Gillian and her brother spent two days in a cottage on Lake Ontario, near to where they were raised— Gillian's map, growing up on Lake Ontario, overlapped with my map—and there they recorded the sounds of the waves lapping on the limestone shore. Being on the ancient lake so soon after her mother died was like a portal to an altered state, she said, where the finite and the infinite seemed to be right next to each other. "Maybe that's what eternity feels like." She sent me the recording, and I remembered my own lake as I listened.

It was a wild place, the lake of my memory. It was often loud with waves that crashed, mostly dark, and always cold. It was where I went to take risks. To run and jump with Meryl on the giant ice floes that rimmed its shore in the snowy winters when we were twelve or thirteen. To kiss a boy. To stay out all night wrapped in that poncho blanket and stare into D's puzzled eyes. You never knew what to expect on the lake, and yet you always knew what to expect because it was constant. It wasn't going anywhere. It waited with its own deep and never-ending story, ready to accept me with my new one. I had come to feel that something essential about myself would be found in my ability to perform the simple act of biking to the lake. Something hidden until now. The idea was so reasonable, and the act so easy to do. It felt unreasonable—obstinate, even—not to.

I practiced a few smaller rides around town on my e-bike. Then I entered the Great Lakes Waterfront Trail route on my phone and attached it to the holder on my handlebars. I folded some Kleenex for the road, plus a small snack, water, sunglasses, sunscreen, and credit cards. As I sat down to tie the laces of my running shoes, I remembered when I would hop on my bike with nothing but my hands and feet to go wherever, for however long. Time changes most things.

"Not a cloud in the sky," I said to myself as I rode under its blue-domed lid on a crisp and shimmering fall morning. It was an amber autumn. The turning leaves were golden and rust instead of red and orange, so less showy than most years. But without the distraction of the bright colors the trees themselves became more noticeable, their branches bravely reaching for the last of the strong sun before it was weakened by the long winter. I was dappled by the light shining through them as I rode my bike south toward the water. I was moving much faster than my physical effort merited. I suppose it was a lot like driving a car. The less work I did, the more I became a passenger. It was a smooth trip on bike paths all the way to the Great Lakes Waterfront Trail, and then—so fast, so fun—I was exactly where I wanted to be. On one side was the pounding lake, as far as I could see, and the other the beautifully treed waterfront park. I rode beside the loud waves with my huge grin and made my way west to Sunnyside Beach, where I got off my bike and sat down by the water. I watched the light touch down on the crests of the waves. I watched the steady lap of the shore. I watched the supercilious ducks who bobbed by as if riding big waves was nothing to them. I looked across the lake to see if I could locate Grimsby on the other side. The way you sometimes can when the sky is clear. Encouraged by the thrilling speed of the e-bike and the beauty of the day, I decided to go further.

ACKNOWLEDGMENTS

PARTS OF A FEW of these chapters have appeared in slightly different form in the *Toronto Star* and in *The Walrus* magazine, and I thank my talented editors at those publications for their encouragement and support.

Thank you to my family and friends, who lived this book along with me, inside and outside its pages.

Kelly Barber

Mary Barber

Ivonne Villatoro

Stefan Barber-Villatoro

Laura Bradbury

Tim Bradbury

David Bradbury

Ann Bradbury

Nancy Keenan

Sam Bradbury

Keogh Dooley

Claire Dooley

Gillian Graham

Tecca Crosby

Johanna Schneller

Ellen Vanstone

Tim Pilgrim

Meryl

D

Thank you to my readers, editors, and counsellors as I wrote.

Ellen Vanstone   Ian Brown
Laura Bradbury   Marni Jackson

Carl Wilson, colleague and friend, author and editor, who has made this book exponentially better.

My agent Jackie Kaiser.

The terrifically talented Penguin Canada team, many behind the scenes, many in front, including: Janice Weaver, my excellent and thoughtful copy editor; Jen Griffiths, who did the cover and design (outside and in); Shona Cook, publicist; the terrific audio team: Jaclyn Gruenberger, producer, and Zak Annette, director; and the practically perfect in every way Lara Hinchberger, my encouraging, present, and unfailingly astute editor.

cred. Mary Barber

CATHRIN BRADBURY worked as a leader and top editor of major Canadian news organizations and magazines for forty years, including as Senior News Director at CBC News, Senior Editor at *Maclean's* magazine, and Managing Editor at *The Globe and Mail*, where she won two National Newspaper Awards for Special Projects. She currently writes features and a column for the *Toronto Star* called "The ¾ Life Crisis," and is a regular contributor to *The Walrus* magazine, where her feature article "The End of Retirement" was nominated for a National Magazine Award in 2024. Her first book, a memoir entitled *The Bright Side*, was published in 2021. She lives in Toronto.

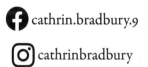

cathrin.bradbury.9

cathrinbradbury